**COMPREHENS**

# CQ

MW01047972

**ISSUE A:** Synthesizing

# Weird and Wonderful

# Weird and Wonderful

## THINK ABOUT: Synthesizing

### A4

FICTION

### Why Cats and Dogs Fight

Have you ever wondered why cats and dogs fight? This Rumanian folktale might have the answer!

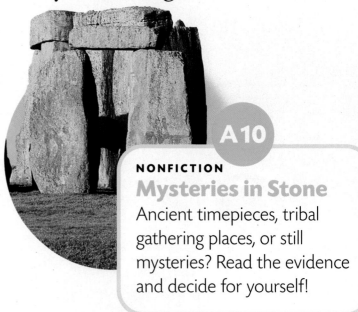

### A10

NONFICTION

### Mysteries in Stone

Ancient timepieces, tribal gathering places, or still mysteries? Read the evidence and decide for yourself!

FICTION

### Odd Aunt Erma Lynn

Do you know anyone who wears two sets of clothes and lives with 12 pigs? Even Lisa isn't sure what to make of her eccentric aunt.

### A18

### A24

NONFICTION

### One for the Record Books

If you've ever dreamed of making or breaking your own world record, you'll be amazed at what others have done!

## In this issue:

### SYNTHESIZING

# It's Clear to Me

When we tell someone about a great movie we just saw, we probably mention the unusual characters, the exotic setting, or the surprising ending. Our reaction to these elements is based on our own personal experience and prior knowledge about the subject of the movie.

The same is true when we read. Whenever we read, we are constantly forming a new idea from the information in each paragraph. For example, when we read a folktale about a certain animal, we might recall our own experiences with that animal or with the lesson of the story. This process is called **synthesizing**.

Sometimes we read a story that is so cool we want to retell it to someone. But retelling a story helps us, too. It helps us clarify important ideas—that is, makes them easier to understand.

Before you retell a story in order to clarify ideas, it sometimes helps to take notes that emphasize the most important parts of the story. You should keep the notes short—sometimes just a word is enough to jog your memory later. When you retell the story, don't give away too much—especially if you want people to read the story for themselves!

Now read "Why Cats and Dogs Fight," the folktale that follows. Use a separate sheet of paper to take notes that capture the most important parts of the story. After you read the story, prepare to retell it by considering this question:

If you were to tell other people about the story you just read, and you could only share a few sentences, what would you tell them?

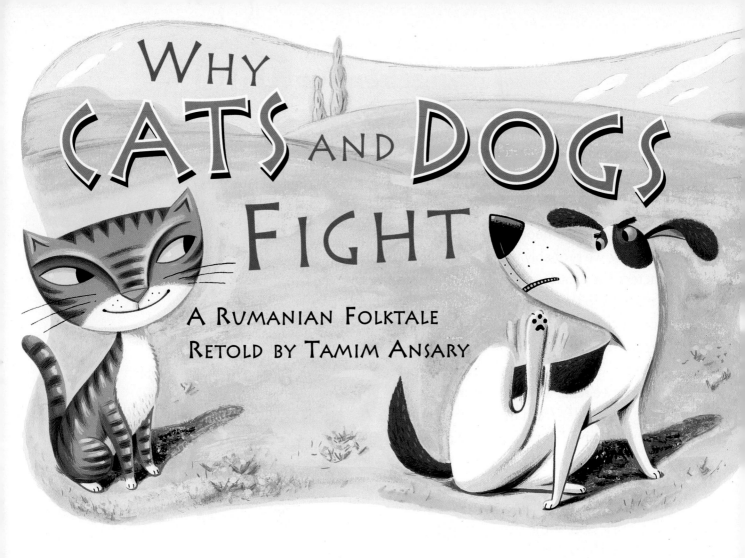

# WHY CATS AND DOGS FIGHT

## A RUMANIAN FOLKTALE
## RETOLD BY TAMIM ANSARY

Long ago, Cat and Dog were friends.

Then Man and Woman came along. The humans planted crops and built a big stone house, and soon they were living a life that made all the animals jealous.

One day, Cat searched out his friend Dog. "Ahoy," said he. "I have an idea."

"I like it already." Dog scratched his side and flapped his ear to shake off a fly. "You're such a clever one, Cat."

Cat bowed modestly. "You'll like it even better when you've heard what it is," he said. "I propose that we go to the humans and offer to become their helpers and companions. In exchange, we'll ask them to keep us well fed all our days. What do you think?"

"It's a fine plan." And to show his admiration, Dog barked nonstop for ten minutes. Then he bounded to his feet and said, "Let's be off at once!"

But Cat said, "Wait a bit. Let us first decide how to divide up the work. For if we don't, the humans will decide for us, and what good is that?"

"Woof," said Dog. "You're right as always, Cat. Tell me then, how shall we divide the work?"

"Well," said Cat, "there is housework and fieldwork. Now, housework is sure to be difficult since we have never been in a house. Why, the inside of a house is to our life as night is to day! But never mind; I will shoulder that

awful job. You take charge of the fields. That should be like chewing on an old bone. After all, we animals are quite familiar with fields and woods. Does that sound fair?"

But Dog was not listening, for he had just spotted something sneaking up on him. He spent the next 15 minutes trying to catch the villain. When he discovered it was his own tail, he returned to Cat, panting hard. "What a workout!" he exclaimed. "You were saying?"

Cat repeated his idea from beginning to end.

"Done," said Dog. "Let's go."

"Not so fast," purred Cat. "Call me persnickety, but I really can't feel comfortable unless things are done properly. Now I have here a contract—"

"A what?" interrupted Dog.

"It's an agreement," Cat snapped. "Everything we talked about is written here in black and white. Read it carefully. If you agree with what it says, sign right here and here and here and here and here and here."

Dog smiled. "What a funny creature you are!" he said. Dog could read, but he only made a show of studying the paper because he didn't enjoy reading. Then he dipped his paws in ink and made his mark everywhere Cat pointed.

Cat signed too, and the friends then made their way to the big house where the humans lived.

Woman and Man listened to Cat's proposal and then offered a counterproposal. The talk went back and forth for quite some time. But Cat held firm, and in the end the humans agreed to all his terms. Dog then took up his post in the fields. Cat made his way into the house.

In one or two sentences, summarize Cat's contract with Dog.

In the days that followed, Dog toiled hard to prove himself. He kept wolves at bay and barked at birds that tried to steal Man's grain. He was out there under the broiling sun, loyally guarding Man's sheep. At night, he slept under a tree with his paws over his nose. When the rain drenched him, he did not complain. Sometimes he even woke up covered with snow. In the old days, he would have found a warm cave in which to defrost himself, but he was on duty now and could not leave the flocks. Through all his troubles, one thing kept him going—the thought of his noble friend Cat and the hardships he must be suffering!

One night, Dog decided to see how Cat was getting along. He made his way to the house.

all the while? Napping and eating! I must say, it doesn't seem quite fair!"

"We all have our sorrows," sighed Cat. "You can't imagine the boredom I suffer. If you had to endure it for one day, believe me, you would be begging to return to your flies and your rain."

"I should like to test that for myself," said Dog. "Let us switch places for a week or two. You take the fields. I will live in the house."

Cat was shocked. "But Dog! We signed a contract. Would you break your promise now? That's not honorable. It may even be illegal!"

"What contract?" woofed Dog.

"Don't you remember that paper we signed?" asked Cat.

"I remember it," said Dog. "But I remember the terms quite differently than you. As I recall it, we agreed to take turns."

"Dog, you are being irresponsible," said Cat. "The contract was quite clear."

"And you are being a big cheater," said Dog.

Cat drew himself up. The one thing he valued above all else was his good name. "I can show you absolute proof—the contract itself, all covered with your paw marks. And what will you say then, eh?"

"If it proves you right, I will grovel before you humbly," said Dog. "But I'm quite sure that won't happen."

"Follow me," Cat huffed. He made his way into the house and up the stairs, step by delicate

As he approached it through the rainy darkness, he saw the warm window full of light. It looked wonderfully inviting! Dog got up on his hind legs to peek over the sill.

And what did he see inside? Why, the coziest little room it is possible to imagine! A fire crackled in the fireplace. The furniture had soft cushions, and on these were piled even softer pillows. And on the softest pillow of all lay Cat, curled up and sleeping peacefully.

Well! Dog could not help but feel a little resentment. And the next time he saw Cat, he spoke sulkily. "There I am outside," he complained, "in every sort of weather, tortured by flies, pounded by rain. And what are you doing

What caused Dog to feel resentment toward Cat? List three things.

step. Dog came gallumphing after. Cat led the way to the attic, where he had hidden the contract carefully under a roof beam.

But when he looked under the beam— horror of horrors! All he saw was a pile of sawdust. Mouse had moved into the house, and he had eaten the contract!

"Well," said Dog. "Where is it?"

Cat stood before Dog, shocked. There was no way to restore his honor now! Then Dog said bitterly, "So this was your ploy! To let Mouse in! And now your lie can never be proven! Why, when I get my jaws on you . . ."

Dog pounced. Cat managed to dash away in time to save his skin. But ever since that day, when Dog sees Cat, the old argument erupts all over again. And when Cat sees Mouse, it's even worse— right to this very day. 🔘

Look back at the notes you took during the story. What were the most important parts? What information would you use to retell this story?

# Stop and Respond

## THE TRUTH ABOUT CATS AND DOGS

The author of "Why Cats and Dogs Fight" exaggerates the characteristics of cats and dogs to make his point—or does he? Are dogs really so devoted? Are cats really more intelligent than dogs? If not, why would the writer describe them that way? Discuss your ideas with a classmate.

## THE ART OF THE STORY

Suppose that the folktale "Why Cats and Dogs Fight" was going to be made into a book for young children. Design and illustrate a colorful book cover that shows the main characters and captures the humor of the story. Use paints, markers, or crayons in the design, and be sure to list yourself as the illustrator.

## ADVANTAGES OF ANIMALS

Many scientists have studied the health benefits of owning cats and dogs, aside from their help in herding sheep and catching field mice. Find some information in the library or on the Internet about how pets help human beings. Prepare a brief report to share with the class.

Most people think of dachshunds, otherwise known as "hot dog dogs," as funny and agreeable pets. However, they were originally bred to fight badgers living in burrows.

Cats might be cuddly and warm, but they are carnivorous killers. Dogs can survive on a vegetarian diet, but cats must have meat.

# carnivorous Cats and Ferocious Dachshunds!

**We may never really know the truth about why cats and dogs fight, but we have learned some amazing facts about the world's two favorite pets.**

Have you ever thought of using a whistle to call your cat? Even though dogs are famous for their ability to hear high-pitched noises, cats actually hear these sounds better.

Not only does the cat frustrate the dog by curling cozily on the couch and leaping easily to high spaces, it lives longer, too! Ten human years equal 70 dog years, but they equal only 60 cat years!

Virtual pets may be one fad that has come and gone, but real pets have stood the test of time. Dogs have been tamed for 100,000 years; the first people to keep cats as pets were the ancient Egyptians, who thought cats were sacred.

# MYSTERIES IN STONE

## by Patricia K. Kummer

Try to imagine living in prehistoric times, thousands of years ago. What do you think prehistoric people ate? How did they dress and make their homes? What dangers did they face? Imagining prehistoric times and the people who lived then is sometimes all we can do. Prehistoric people did not leave a written record of their lives and times for us to read. In fact, *prehistoric* means the time before people started to record history in written form.

So how can we know anything about life in prehistoric times? We rely on archaeologists—scientists who investigate the lives of early people by studying the objects they left behind. These include buildings, or parts of buildings, drawings, bones, and objects such as tools, pottery, and toys. By looking at some of this evidence, archaeologists have figured out that prehistoric people used only very simple tools and that they did not write down plans for buildings.

Thinking about those two facts, it is amazing to learn that prehistoric people actually managed to build huge stone monuments. And parts of many of these monuments still stand today, more than 5,000 years later! Stonehenge and the Easter Island moai are only two examples of the determination of prehistoric people.

Even though archaeologists think they know the age of these two amazing prehistoric sites, many mysteries remain. Who built these sites? How did they move the stones for the monuments? Why did they build them? By studying evidence left behind, archaeologists think they know what might have happened. But they continue to dig into the past for even more evidence that will help them solve some of the mysteries surrounding these special monuments.

What two facts make Stonehenge and the Easter Island moai so amazing?

# STONEHENGE

Standing along a modern highway in southern England is a sight that can almost instantly remind visitors of times long past. That sight is Stonehenge. A group of huge, rough-cut stones set in circles, Stonehenge is perhaps the best-known prehistoric stone monument on Earth.

## Building Stonehenge

Archaeologists think prehistoric people built Stonehenge in three phases, or steps. In the first phase, they dug a circular ditch, or *henge*. It was 1,000 feet around, 20 feet wide, and 6 feet deep—making it larger than an entire football field. What makes this digging even more remarkable is that these ancient people did not use bulldozers and earth movers to make this giant ditch. The only tools they had were deer antlers and sharpened animal bones!

Once the ditch was finished, the builders used the leftover rock and soil to make an earthen wall. Inside this wall, they dug 56 holes.

As you read about the building of Stonehenge, take notes about the three different phases and what happened during each one.

But even then, they weren't done working! They built an opening in the ditch that led to a wide path. In the center of the path, they placed a large, 16-foot tall stone.

The people who were building Stonehenge stopped working on it for about 500 years. Then its second building phase began. These later builders set up 80 stone pillars in two circles, one inside the other. Each of these stones weighed about 4 tons. They came from an area about 240 miles away from Stonehenge. How did these ancient people get these mammoth stones from so far away? Some archaeologists think they floated the stones down rivers and then used sleds on log rollers to move them to Stonehenge.

Then work on Stonehenge stopped for about another 100 years. In the third and final phase of building, Stonehenge was totally changed. This last group of builders faced a challenge greater than any of the previous builders. They moved even larger stones more than 20 miles using a sled on log rollers! Then they set up these huge stones, called *sarsens,* in a large circle between the original ditch and the second ring of stones. Each sarsen weighed between 25 and 40 tons, or as much as 11 minivans. Compare this to an African bull elephant, the largest land mammal, which weighs about 7 tons. The builders arranged 10 of the taller sarsens in the shape of a horseshoe. Then they arranged 19 of the stone pillars from the second phase into a smaller horseshoe inside the sarsens. Finally, Stonehenge was completed. Altogether, the construction of Stonehenge took about *30 million hours* and *hundreds of years* to complete.

> Now in a few sentences, summarize the key information about each phase in the building of Stonehenge.

## Why All the Hard Work?

Scientists have different ideas about why prehistoric people built Stonehenge. Some scientists think Stonehenge was built as a tribal gathering place. Others think that would have been a lot of work for a neighborhood meeting! Some researchers think the monument was built for religious reasons, and some believe Stonehenge was simply built as a monument.

In recent years, some people have proposed another reason why Stonehenge was built and what it was used for. Astronomers—scientists who study the sun, the moon, the stars and the planets—believe that the sun shines through the spaces between the stones at a special angle on the

Scientists who study outer space believe that Stonehenge is a huge astronomical calendar.

longest and shortest days of the year. For this reason, scientists believe that the placement of the stones at Stonehenge helps predict the coming of the seasons.

Another reason scientists believe Stonehenge was used as a calendar is that the 56 holes dug during the first phase can be used to measure the cycle of the moon. By moving a marker two holes each day for 28 days, prehistoric people could have followed a complete cycle of the moon. Astronomers also think other stones in the monument helped prehistoric people predict eclipses of the sun and the moon. Some astronomers think this is strong evidence that Stonehenge was as important to prehistoric people as calendars are to us today!

> What do you understand now about prehistoric people that you didn't understand before?

## Stonehenge Today

Today, only part of the original Stonehenge still stands. Through the centuries, wind and rain have worn down the surfaces of the stones, and many of the stones have been taken to build houses, farm buildings, and bridges. More recently, thoughtless tourists have taken chips from the stones. But in 1986, Stonehenge became a World Heritage Site. It is now protected, and hopefully, it will remain a weird and wonderful mystery to delight and puzzle many generations to come.

# EASTER ISLAND

On the other side of the world from Stonehenge lies Easter Island. Easter Island is a small island in the South Pacific Ocean that was formed by three volcanoes. Though the island was discovered on Easter Sunday in 1722 by Dutch explorers, archaeologists believe that other people had explored the island as early as 300 A.D.

The Dutch sailors only stayed on Easter Island for a few hours, but they had time to notice the giant *moai,* or statues, on the island. "Moai" means "image" to the islanders. Archaeologists agree that there may have been as many as 600 moai originally, but at the time of the visit by the Dutch explorers, only 288 remained. When the English explorer Captain James Cook arrived on the island in 1774, most of the moai had been knocked down. Many experts think the islanders had had a war, and the statues were damaged during the fighting.

## Building the Moai

Between about 700 and 1600 A.D., the natives of Easter Island built about 900 moai. Using pointed stone picks, the islanders carved the moai from volcanic rock. Although the statues are not identical, they all have a similar look: long heads on a thick body with thin arms held tightly to their sides. Moai hands rest on their stomachs. Their faces have deep-set eyes, long earlobes, and slightly jutting chins. Some moai have a crown, or topknot, on their heads. The statues range in height from 6 to 32 feet and weigh from 10 to 84 tons. That means that the largest one weighs as much as 12 elephants!

Archaeologists believe the moai were brought from a volcano's crater to the shore on sleds similar to the ones used by people who built Stonehenge. Each year, archaeologists find more moai near island trails. According to Captain Cook, the islanders told him that the moai represented their chiefs, and that the moai all face away from the sea to better guard the inland villages.

> What information have you learned about the Easter Island moai?

## The Moai Today

Since the 1950s, the natives of Easter Island and groups of archaeologists have worked to restore and raise many of the fallen moai. In 1955, Easter Island became a World Heritage Site with the hope that these unique monuments would be protected from further harm.

## Stonehenge and the Moai: Different Yet Similar

England's Stonehenge and the moai on Easter Island were built in different times and places, but they share many similarities. Both were constructed from enormous stones. Thousands of miles and years apart, these two ancient peoples pulled the pieces of their monuments on sleds over greased pathways. Many stones have fallen or been pushed down from both sites, but now each place is protected from further damage. And finally, both Stonehenge and the moai of Easter Island are tributes to the people who constructed them. Using the simplest tools, these determined people built unique, magnificent monuments that continue to amaze the world. ◉

> Using a graphic organizer such as a Venn diagram, list the similarities and differences between Stonehenge and the Easter Island moai.

# Stop and Respond

## Weigh in on Stonehenge

What do you think Stonehenge was used for? Was it an ancient calendar or a tribal gathering place? Use information from the article as well as information you find on the Internet to support your opinion. Write a few paragraphs in your journal explaining your thoughts.

## Unanswered Questions

Many unanswered questions remain about Stonehenge and the Easter Island moai. What would you like to know? With a partner, develop a list of questions you'd like answered, and the resources you would consult to find this information.

## History, Fiction, or Both?

Chances are, the real truth about Stonehenge and the Easter Island moai might be stranger than fiction. Use the facts—and your imagination—to create a short story about either Stonehenge or Easter Island. Set your story during one of the time periods described in the article. Illustrate your story and share it with the class.

# See Amazing
# CHIRICAHUA
## Nature's Stonehenge

The United States might not have an archaeological site as ancient or as mysterious as Stonehenge, but it has something close. If you travel through the forests along the snakelike Bonita Canyon Drive in Willcox, Arizona, you'll find yourself in the "Land of Standing-up Rocks."

Unlike the giant rocks of Stonehenge, these formations were not created by people. Geologists believe that about 27 million years ago, a nearby volcano erupted and a **caldera** spewed out thick white-hot ash. When the ash cooled, it hardened into an almost 2,000-foot-thick layer of volcanic rock. This rock upheaval also formed the Chiricahua Mountains. Gradually, water, wind, and ice sculpted the rock into unusual formations. This same kind of erosion carved cracks that helped to form the amazing upright rock formations preserved in the Chiricahua National Monument.

The park has more than 20 miles of trails, which wind past such unusually named rocks as Duck on a Rock, Totem Pole, and Big Balanced Rock. They also lead to a small natural bridge and a ledge created by the same volcanic eruption.

(above left) Big Balanced Rock, (left) Rock Pinnacles at Chiricahua

**caldera:** a volcanic crater formed by a violent explosion

## SYNTHESIZING

# Just the Facts

As you recall from the activity on page A3, one way to **synthesize** what you read is to retell it to someone else. Retelling the story helps you clarify the important parts.

All the details about Stonehenge made it difficult for Kyra to keep track of the important points in "Mysteries in Stone." So she wrote the following paragraph to clarify the key information in her own mind.

Read Kyra's paragraph at right. Notice that she includes only basic information about Stonehenge. This helps her grasp the main ideas about the subject. Later, she might write other paragraphs that focus on different parts of Stonehenge, such as the different building phases or why it was built.

The next time you read something, clarify its most important ideas by retelling it to someone you know. Not only will you better understand what you read, you'll share some interesting information with your friend.

Stonehenge is a group of huge stones set in circles in England. It was built in three phases. In the first phase, a ditch was dug. In the second phase, stones were arranged in two circles, one inside the other. In the last phase, giant stones were added. No one knows for sure why Stonehenge was built. Some people think that it was designed as a tribal gathering place. Others say it is a giant astrological calendar. That is because at certain times of the year, the stones line up with the sunrise.

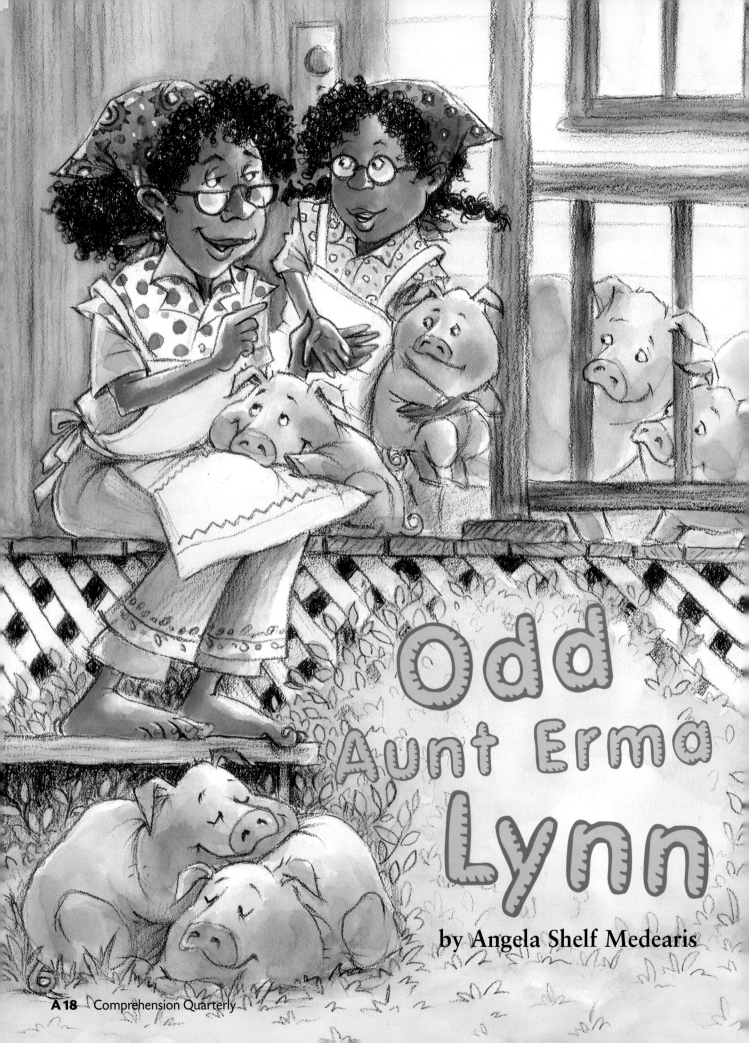

# Odd
# Aunt Erma
# Lynn

by Angela Shelf Medearis

Summertime means one thing to me—I get to visit my Aunt Erma Lynn. She lives in the super-small town of Tinsel, Texas. The nearest doctor is in Cold Spring, about 120 miles away. But no one who needs a doctor around Tinsel seems to mind visiting Aunt Erma Lynn instead, because she is hyperefficient and a professionally trained physician's assistant. She has an odd way of doing things and never used to smile, but she's always been kind to everyone.

When people are sick, Aunt Erma Lynn examines them from head to toe. At other times, she just looks at patients' hands while they talk about their problems. Whenever a patient asks Aunt Erma Lynn to explain her nursing methods, she just pouts and flounces out of the room. Most folks don't ask her any questions— they just keep talking a mile a minute.

One evening, I finally got up the courage to ask Aunt Erma Lynn about her nursing methods. She just frowned and said, "Sometimes people aren't really sick. They just need to talk about their problems. Holding their hands while I listen to them talk takes their minds off their shyness."

Synthesize what you have read so far. Think of five ways to describe Aunt Erma Lynn.

When Aunt Erma Lynn figures out what's wrong with her sick patients, she starts making her supersecret, hypoallergenic, herbal Sure-Enough-Cure-All-Stuff. She picks a bunch of herbs and boils them in a pot. Then she puts in a pinch of this and a handful of that.

"Lisa," Aunt Erma Lynn once said while she stirred the Stuff, "please get out the mayo, some veggie burgers, some whole-wheat bread, a sour pickle, and some brownies."

"Are you going to put those ingredients into the Stuff?" I asked.

"No, silly," Aunt Erma Lynn said. "That food is for our brunch."

Aunt Erma Lynn and I spend most summers in the woods looking for the herbs that go into her medicines. She always wears two pairs of cotton drawstring pants, two blouses, two pairs of socks, and an apron with big pockets.

"Why do you wear all those clothes in the summer?" I finally asked. "You look funny."

By the look in her eyes, I could tell I'd hurt her feelings. Oh, sometimes I wish I could just keep my big mouth shut.

"Layering my clothes saves time if someone's sick," Aunt Erma Lynn said after a long silence. "If something gets dirty, all I have to do is take it off and I'm clean again. Then I can see the next patient without delay."

"Oh, that makes sense," I said.

I decided to try Aunt Erma Lynn's way of dressing to make up for what I'd said. I found out that big apron pockets are perfect for carrying everything you need. And all the layers of clothes are thin cotton, so I don't get hot. Aunt Erma Lynn's way of dressing is a good idea.

Aunt Erma Lynn is the only person I know who lives with 12 pigs. I used to hide whenever someone came to the house when I was there because I didn't want anyone to know that Aunt Erma Lynn and I are related. Then I noticed how sad Aunt Erma Lynn looked whenever I ducked into my room as the doorbell rang. It made me feel bad.

Besides, everyone already knows about the pigs and that she and I are in the same family. Everyone in Tinsel tells us that we act alike, too. I used to hate it when people said that—until I noticed how much Aunt Erma Lynn's nursing helps people. From that day on, I decided to be proud of the fact that Aunt Erma Lynn is one of the best physician's assistants in Texas. Now when we have visitors, I just move the pigs off the couch and make our guests feel at home.

What caused Lisa to be embarrassed by her Aunt Erma Lynn?

When I'm not helping my aunt, I like to go fishing down by the river with Miss Prissy, Aunt Erma Lynn's favorite piglet. The only bad thing about going fishing is that I have to walk past the old Morgan house. Some folks around here say the place is haunted. Of course, I'm not scared of passing that old house. I keep telling myself that running at top speed with a lunch pail, a bait bucket, a fishing pole, and a pig in your apron pocket is just good exercise.

One day, I was nearly past that old house when I tripped on a tree root. Miss Prissy and I were suddenly airborne. Half-eaten sandwiches and worms flew everywhere! When I landed, I banged my head against the tree. While I was lying there, a big fat worm crawled out of my hair. "Yuck," I said, brushing it away. Three more wigglers were crawling down my back. I was covered with worms. I danced around, wiggling and kicking up so much dirt underneath that tree that it looked like a dust storm. By the time I got the last worm off me, I was covered with dirt.

It was a good thing I was dressed like Aunt Erma Lynn. I took off the dirty blouse and pants. My clothes underneath were still clean. I smiled. Aunt Erma Lynn might be a little odd, but she has some good ideas from time to time.

I was reaching down to pick up my fishing pole when something shiny caught my eye. It was buried near the tree root where I'd tripped. I found a stick and started digging. Finally I was able to pry it out of the ground. It was a jar full of money! I couldn't believe my eyes. "I'm super-rich!" I said softly. Then I looked around, stuck the jar in my lunch pail, picked up my pole and bucket, and ran for Aunt Erma Lynn's house. I burst through the kitchen door so fast I almost knocked her down.

"What in the world is wrong with you?" Aunt Erma Lynn asked. "Did you see something scary?"

"No, Ma'am," I panted. I pulled the jar out of the pail.

"My gracious, Lisa!" said Aunt Erma Lynn. "Where did you get all that money?"

"I found it when I fell down and bumped my head outside the old Morgan house," I said.

Aunt Erma Lynn looked at the bump on my forehead. She made me swallow some Stuff. Yuck! But at least my head stopped hurting.

"Can I keep the money, Aunt Erma Lynn?" I pleaded. "Finders, keepers!"

"Not always, Lisa," Aunt Erma Lynn said. "But it's finders, keepers this time. Mr. Morgan didn't have any relatives left, and no one has ever claimed his land or other property."

"Yippee!" I hollered. "I'm rich!"

"You'd better count the money before you start claiming you're rich," Aunt Erma Lynn said.

I did count every last dollar, and I stacked it into piles, too. "It's $2,989.76!" I whooped.

Aunt Erma Lynn's birthday was the next day. Now I could buy her a really nice present.

"Aunt Erma Lynn," I said, "I want to buy you something really special for your birthday."

"Well, that's sweet of you," said Aunt Erma Lynn, thinking it over. "To tell you the truth, I've always wanted to get my teeth fixed."

I couldn't stop myself from exclaiming "*Teeth?* You want some *teeth* for a birthday present?"

Then I suddenly realized why my aunt never smiled. She was ashamed of her teeth. "Well," I said, "maybe we could go to Cold Spring tomorrow. I'll bet the dentist could make some false teeth for you."

"Thank you," said Aunt Erma Lynn. "This will be one of the best birthday presents I've ever had."

How has Lisa changed during the course of the story? How does this affect your synthesis of the story?

Later, after a few weeks of sore gums, Aunt Erma Lynn became adjusted to her new teeth. They were as white as a pearl necklace. And from the moment she was able to chew comfortably, Aunt Erma Lynn began eating the toughest steaks, crunching peanut brittle, tearing into taffy, and chomping hard, green apples. One time, she ate so much that I had to give her a dose of Stuff and then help her into bed. I also picked a bunch of bright yellow mums and put them in a jar by her bed.

"You're going to be a wonderful doctor someday, Lisa," Aunt Erma Lynn said as I tucked her in, and then she smiled at me. Her shiny teeth twinkled in the moonlight as she drifted off to sleep. And I think mine twinkled, too. ⬤

Did your thinking about Aunt Erma Lynn change during the story? Why or why not?

Of course, I started dreaming about all the things I was going to buy. That is, until Aunt Erma Lynn burst my bubble. "Lisa," Aunt Erma Lynn said, "do you remember that you told me you want to go to medical school and be a doctor? If you save that money, you can use it for your education."

My dreams of a weekend at the mall began to fade away. "What if I save most of it and spend the rest?" I asked.

"Oh, all right," Aunt Erma Lynn said.

I counted out a third of the money and put the rest of it back into the jar. Aunt Erma Lynn hid the money on the top shelf of the linen closet until we could get to the bank.

I looked at the money I had left and started dreaming again. That is, until I remembered that

# Stop and Respond

## An Ode to Oddity

Aunt Erma Lynn is the only person Lisa knows who lives with 12 pigs. Is there someone you know who is eccentric or wonderfully weird? Compose a poem about that person. Be as descriptive as possible!

## Fun in the Summertime

In the opening paragraph of the story, Lisa says "Summertime means one thing to me—I get to visit my Aunt Erma Lynn." What unusual activity or person do you associate with summer? In your journal, write a few paragraphs to complete the sentence "Summertime means one thing to me—"

## You Cannot Buy Love

One thousand dollars would buy a lot of CDs, video games, or cool shoes. Were you surprised by the way in which Lisa spent her money? Think of a loved one whose birthday is approaching. Create a top-ten list of inexpensive—but priceless—gifts you could give that person to show your love. Then consider actually giving the person one of the gifts on your list.

# One for the Record Books

by Maureen Mecozzi

The biggest, the smallest, the longest, the shortest . . . it seems we always want to know who or what has made it to "the top"! Who's the fastest? Who's the slowest? What's the highest? Where's the lowest?

But why? Why are we so thrilled by **extremes?** What inspired Angelica Unverhau of Dinslaken, Germany, to write herself into the record books as the proud owner of the World's Biggest Ballpoint Pen Collection—168,700 pens at the last count! What prompted the people of Selinsgrove, Pennsylvania, to dish out 4 miles and 965 yards of ice cream, bananas, whipped cream, and cherries to claim the title of World's Longest Banana Split?

Some people aim for world records just for recognition. It's a way to be noticed and stand out from the crowd. Others want to challenge themselves and do what everyone says can't be done.

For many, though, it's the challenge alone that's enough. When Sir George Mallory was asked why he tried to scale Mount Everest, the world's highest mountain (29,028 feet), he said simply, "Because it's there."

Whether people, places, or animals, the world's **superlatives** grab our attention. Read on and be amazed!

What are some of the things that make people want to set world records?

# It Started with Sports

You could say that keeping track of excellence in human effort began with sports. Athletic games were an important part of daily life in ancient Greece, and people with extraordinary skill were greatly admired.

The serious business of keeping sports records began with the modern Olympic Games in 1896. Achievements were recorded using tape measures, stopwatches, and photos. Judges for different sports set the standards and kept records. Today, the Olympics is one of thousands of sports competitions in which athletes aim to outdo their rivals and set a standard that can't be topped.

But enough about *keeping* sports records. Who actually *makes* them?

The title of "World's Fastest Human," always a hotly contested claim, currently goes to the American sprinter, Maurice Greene. He ran 100 meters at the blisteringly fast pace of 9.79 seconds in June 1999. Greene took .05 seconds off the previous record, the biggest margin since electronic timing was introduced in the 1960s. Greene holds several other track speed records as well. "The world record is very important," Greene said before his famous race. "But I can't go after the world record. I have to run the world-record race and not race the world record."

The youngest person to win a gold medal at the Olympics was Dominique Moceanu, a member of the U.S. gymnastics team. At the 1996 Olympic games in Atlanta, Georgia, young Dominique was only 14 years old on the day she stood with her teammates to be honored for their achievement.

Who has the fastest serve in women's tennis? The current answer is Venus Williams, who's capable of hitting the ball 127.4 miles per hour. And Nolan Ryan whipped baseball's fastest pitch

(left) Venus Williams holds the world's record for fastest serve in women's tennis. (right) Nolan Ryan served baseball's fastest pitch ever in 1974.

past an unsuspecting batter in 1974. It whizzed by at 100.9 miles per hour. No one has been able to beat that record since.

The World's Longest Footrace covered a distance of 3,665 miles, from New York City to Los Angeles, California. Held in 1929, it took Finnish winner Johnny Salo 79 long, tiring days to finish. Jack Smith decided to speed things up a bit in 1984—he crossed the U.S.A. on a *skateboard* in only 26 days! Identical twins Nick and Alastair Benbow of the United Kingdom ran the 1998 World's Fastest Three-Legged Marathon in London. The twins tied their wrists together and each stuck one leg into the middle of a specially-made three-legged pair of running pants. The Benbows finished the race in 3 hours, 40 minutes, 16 seconds. Talk about teamwork!

Captain Alan Shepard, commander of the *Apollo 14* spacecraft, holds an *interplanetary* sports record: He was the first man to play golf on the moon! His drive traveled 200 yards because it was aided by the moon's reduced gravity.

What are three things you have learned about world records in sports?

*eeww*

Mark Hogg set a new world record (and spoiled a lot of appetites!) when he swallowed 62 live nightcrawlers in 1998.

## Fantabulous Foods and Meals

Many world records involve food and eating, perhaps because we enjoy stretching the boundaries of the simple things we do every day.

Frenchman Michel Lotito calls himself Monsieur Mangetout (Mr. Eat-All), and with good reason. He's eaten supermarket carts, TVs, aluminum skis, coins, bicycles—of which he says the chain is the tastiest part—and even an airplane! Lotito cuts the objects into small pieces with a power saw and eats about 2 pounds of metal a day. It took him about 2 years to consume the plane, a Cessna 150. Doctors discovered that the linings of Mr. Lotito's stomach and intestines are about twice the thickness of the average human's, which is why he is able to eat objects that would be fatal to other people. Mailboxes are a real treat for the Man Who Has Eaten the Most Metal, but he has a hypersensitivity to soft foods, such as eggs and bananas.

In 1998, Mark Hogg of Louisville, Kentucky, ate 62 live nightcrawlers in 30 seconds to claim the Most Creepy Crawlies Eaten record. He says that his technique is tilting his head back, letting the worm squiggle a little, and then swallowing it whole. This may sound weirdly disgusting, but worms contain more protein than chicken or tuna.

If you're ever stuck in Antarctica and hungry for a snack, you might try calling Eagle Boys Dial-a-Pizza in Christchurch, New Zealand. The pizza parlor regularly delivers to Scott Base, Antarctica, for New Zealand researchers studying the cold continent. The pizzas are cooked, packed, shipped to an airfield, loaded onto a plane, and delivered to the base nine hours later with reheating instructions. It's the World's Longest Pizza Delivery!

Towns and villages around the world often get into record books by cooking up something BIG. Folks in Seymour, Wisconsin, grilled the

Look out below!!!

World's Biggest Burger—a whopping 2.5 tons—in the summer of 1989. In 1995, the Longest Continuous Sausage stretched a distance of 28 miles and 1,354 yards in Kitchener, Ontario. Three years later, in Alberta, Canada, the World's Biggest Ice Cream Sundae weighed in at 22.59 tons. That supersweet treat included 18.38 tons of ice cream and 3.98 tons of syrup.

> In just a few sentences, summarize some of the world records involving food.

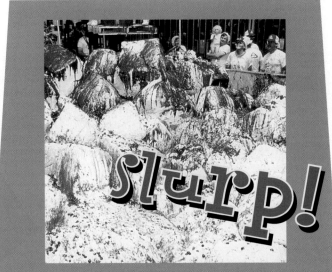

Leave room for dessert! Pictured is the world's largest sundae, weighing in at more than 22 tons!

## Set Your Own Record

Not everyone can break a time barrier in a 100-meter race or own the world's most expensive painting. But there are many kinds of world records set every day by people who just want to have some fun, gain a little fame, and do some good in the process.

Twelve-year-old Ryan Tripp of Utah wanted to help a sick child in his hometown who needed a liver transplant. Ryan found sponsors and then rode a lawn mower 3,366 miles from Salt Lake City, Utah, to Washington, D.C., in the summer of 1997. During the 42-day trip, Ryan took roads approved by the police and followed a lead car driven by members of his family. He raised more than $15,000 and won a place in the record books for the World's Longest Lawn Mower Ride.

The "Lawn Mower Boy" didn't stop there, however. Ryan wanted to raise awareness about the need for organ donations by mowing the lawn of every state capitol in the United States within 75 days. On August 9, 1999, he achieved his goal and racked up another world record. Ryan met many people across the country during his record-setting attempts, including governors and U.S. senators. And millions of people learned about Ryan's quest when he appeared on a late-night TV program. You never know where a lawn mower can take you!

> What led Ryan Tripp to set his two world records?

roarr

Shown is the World's Longest Dancing Dragon, which measured 1 mile and 936 yards.

Many people set records simply by starting collections, like Sweden's Ove Nordstrom, who owns the World's Most Piggy Banks. Other people join group challenges, like the 3,760 people in Hong Kong who created the World's Longest Dancing Dragon, which measured a record 1 mile, 936 yards. Record-setting teams have danced in **conga lines,** linked paper clip chains, set up millions of dominoes—and even jumped into the record of Longest Leapfrog (996 miles and 292 yards—achieved by 14 Stanford University students in 1991).

If your record-setting attempt is interesting, is safe, requires skill, and might attract future challenges from others, you, too, may have a chance to make it into the record books. So go for it! ○

## Glossary

**extremes:** the greatest, highest, farthest; going beyond the norm
**superlatives:** superior to all others
**conga lines:** a Latin American dance in which the dancers form a long, winding line

your name HERE!

## Book of School Superlatives

Record books don't have to include only athletic ability, odd appetites, or unusual size. They can also provide fascinating information about the people around you. For example, do you know which of your teachers has taught at your school the longest? Which of your classmates has read the most books during the past month? Who has the most unusual collection? With your class, conduct a survey that answers questions like these. If you want, you can gather the information in a *Book of School Superlatives* to show off at the next Open House.

# Stop and Respond

## News Flash!

Choose one of the amazing records described in the story. Check out the *Guinness Book of World Records* or some Internet newspaper archives to get more information about the feat. Write a news article about the event as if you witnessed it yourself. Remember to answer the questions *who, what, when, where,* and *why* in your story. Top it off with an attention-grabbing headline.

## Breaking Records for Charity

You've heard of walkathons, dance-athons, and other events in which participants test their stamina to raise money for a charity. The amount of money each participant raises depends on how long he or she performs the activity. Think of a worthy cause in your community. Next, as a class, brainstorm fundraising ideas that involve breaking a local record of some kind—think of activities that people your age do a lot of anyway— like reading books, shoveling snow, or mowing lawns. Create a flyer about the event that includes important information and fun graphics.

## Let's Write

## Stranger Than Fiction?

In science-fiction stories, writers take real scientific facts and twist them to make weird and wonderful tales. Sci-fi writers create worlds in which UFOs, mutant animals, and futuristic fantasies amaze and excite us. Think about some intriguing facts you've learned this year in science. Use one or two of them to tap into your own weird and wonderful ideas. Then use them to create a short science-fiction story.

## Exotic Pets

From ferrets to skunks to tarantulas—some people have unusual choices in pets. Do some research to find out about one "weird" pet. Write a short list of the creature's special needs, habits, and care instructions. What would be fun about having such an unusual pet? What about your pet could make it difficult to keep (such as its adult size or its feeding requirements)?

## Weirdsville, U.S.A.

Create a brochure about weird and wonderful places to visit in your own town. The places can be real or imagined. Write inviting, descriptive text, and illustrate your brochure to capture the flavor of some of the places you describe.

## A Twisted Explanation

Write your own folktale to explain an unusual happening, such as why socks disappear in the dryer, why cats climb trees, or why dogs chase their tails. Use "Why Cats and Dogs Fight" as a model for your work.

## More Books

Ganeri, Anita. *Bizarre Beast: And Other Oddities of Nature (series)*. McClanahan Book Co., 1999.

Lorens, Albert. *Buried Blueprints: Maps and Sketches of Lost Worlds and Mysterious Places*. Harry N. Abrams, 1999.

Vande Velde, Vivian. *Tales from Brothers Grimm and Sisters Weird*. Bantam Books, 1997.

## On the Web

**Weird and Wonderful Places to Visit**
http://www.roadsideamerica.com

**More about Stonehenge**
http://www.exn.ca/mysticplaces/
    stonehenge.cfm

**Minerals and Rocks**
http://library.thinkquest.org/J002744/
    adlm.html

**Odd Facts from
Ripley's Believe It or Not**
http://www.ripleys.com

## Across the Curriculum

### Art

For years, artists have used color, form, and shape to stretch the way we view the world. Find an art book and select an artist whose work interests you. For example, you might find the works of Erté, Pablo Picasso, or Salvador Dali wonderfully weird. Choose one artist and create your own piece of art in his or her style.

### Social Studies

Research some weird and wonderful places to visit in the United States, such as Carhenge in Alliance, Nebraska; the world's largest bug in Providence, Rhode Island; or the mysterious Oregon Vortex in Gold Hill, Oregon. List information about that place, along with a picture, on a large index card. With the class, use the cards to create a tour book of weird and wonderful places in the United States.

# EYE POPPING OPTICAL ILLUSIONS

Optical illusions are images that appear to show one thing—until you look more closely, that is! Then you find that the picture shows something completely different. Check out these weird and wonderful images. Answer the question next to each one. Are you amazed by the answer? Check out more cool optical illusions on the Internet or at the library.

**1.**

Which of the horizontal lines are longer, the top one or the bottom one?

**2.** Which step is the bottom and which is the top?

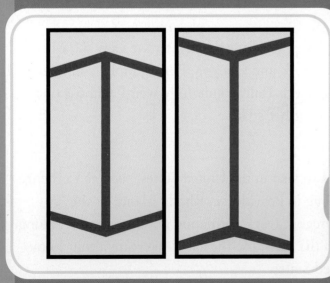

**3.**

Which vertical line is longer?

**COMPREHENSION QUARTERLY** 5

# CQ

**ISSUE B:** Synthesizing

# Short Stuff

# THE MYSTERY OF THE FLASHING LIGHTS

## by Tim Arnold

### Short flashing lights, hoofprints, an eerie story... what could it all mean?

Davis Bell sat up and yawned. He was puzzled by the strangeness of the dark shapes around him. Nothing looked right. It was night, long past midnight, he guessed. Then his head cleared enough to remember that he was in a tent on Cape Cod, in a sleeping bag, not at home or even in the old RV. Lying to his right was his sister, Liz. On his left was his mother, and on *her* left was his dad, all sound asleep. Davis sat up just long enough to realize that he would like very much to be asleep again, like everyone else. Just before he lay back down, he saw short flashes of light off to the right of the tent. A beam of light was on for a couple of seconds, then off for what seemed like five or six. Then on, then off. The whole sequence lasted just a few minutes.

"Oh, right," thought Davis, "the lighthouse." And then he lay down and went back to sleep.

When the tent glowed with the light of morning, he heard and smelled breakfast being cooked. That would be Dad. Dad always got up early on these camping trips

and fixed things they normally didn't eat, like corned beef hash. Liz sat up next to him and stretched.

"I slept really well," she murmured happily. "I was *so* tired."

They had arrived only the day before, and after setting up camp, had spent the rest of the day swimming, body surfing, and flying kites with their summer friends, Paul and Rennie McGill. Paul was 15, the same age as Liz, and Rennie (short for Renata) was 12, same as Davis. Their families had found each other five summers ago. They had met on the beach and everybody had enjoyed everybody, parents included, so they had started reserving adjacent campsites at the same time every summer. They were together one short week out of every year.

"*I* didn't sleep so well," grumbled Davis. "I woke up in the middle of the night and saw the lighthouse flashing over there . . . " and he waved over to the right.

"You mean over *there*," corrected Liz, pointing left. "That's where the lighthouse is. You must have been dreaming."

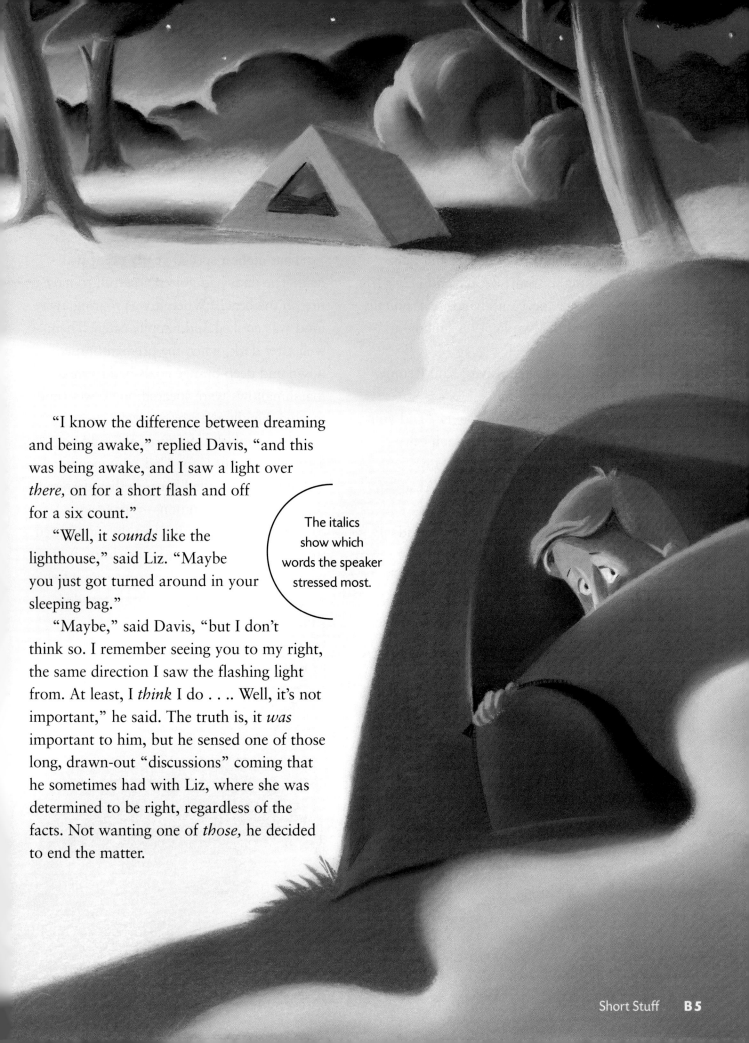

"I know the difference between dreaming and being awake," replied Davis, "and this was being awake, and I saw a light over *there,* on for a short flash and off for a six count."

"Well, it *sounds* like the lighthouse," said Liz. "Maybe you just got turned around in your sleeping bag."

The italics show which words the speaker stressed most.

"Maybe," said Davis, "but I don't think so. I remember seeing you to my right, the same direction I saw the flashing light from. At least, I *think* I do . . .. Well, it's not important," he said. The truth is, it *was* important to him, but he sensed one of those long, drawn-out "discussions" coming that he sometimes had with Liz, where she was determined to be right, regardless of the facts. Not wanting one of *those,* he decided to end the matter.

Later that day, Liz, Paul, Davis, and Rennie were walking on the beach together. They had only to walk a quarter-mile from the campground, on a path through some woods, to reach the beach. Liz and Paul were walking in front. Rennie and Davis noted that Liz and Paul's hands occasionally brushed, and the two kept on smiling at each other.

"That is really repulsive," said Rennie. "*We'll* never be like that."

"That's for sure," said Davis. "Did you know they've been *e-mailing* each other?"

"Of course," said Rennie. "How could I not? I saw one signed SWAK. *Really* repulsive."

"Hey, look here!" cried Davis suddenly. "Hoofprints!" There were, in fact, hoofprints in the sand up above the high tide mark. They ran for just a short distance and then stopped. Liz and Paul turned.

"Those are hoofprints all right," agreed Liz casually.

"Well, isn't that a little unusual?" asked Davis.

"Nah," said Paul. "People are always riding horses around here."

"But on the beach?" asked Rennie.

"Sure," said Liz. The two turned and started walking and chatting again.

> How does the dialogue help you get to know the characters?

"You know," said Rennie, "I can't stand being a chaperone."

"Me neither," agreed Davis. And the two ran off down the beach.

That night a special yearly event was held. The dads had gotten a permit to have a fire on the beach. When it was roaring away, food was cooked and happily eaten. Then, well after dark, when the fire had burned down and deep-orange coals had formed, marshmallows were speared on skewers and toasted. Finally the stories began.

Mom took the last turn, and told an eerie story about Cape Cod "mooncussers" of long ago, so-called because they despised the presence of the moon—it gave sea captains light to see by when they navigated the dangerous waters near the shore. It was well known, she said, that some scoundrels would take advantage of storm-stranded ships and strip them of their cargo as soon as they knew the crew was safe— or drowned. But the real "mooncussers," she said in a low whisper, were shadowy

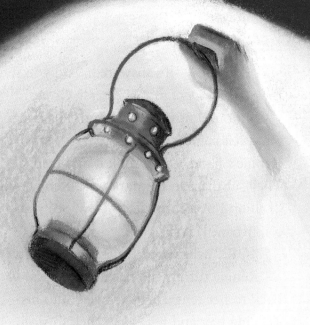

figures who purposefully misled the sailors to crash upon the rocks. They rode the beaches on horseback on dark or stormy nights and used bright lanterns to mimic the pulse of light from lighthouses in order to confuse ships into grounding on the rocks, where their crews were *murdered* and the cargo plundered.

When Mom finished, everyone shivered. The fire was put out and the families gathered their belongings. The walk back through the woods was lit only by two dim flashlights. Everyone was quiet in the semidarkness. Fog crept in on a cool breeze and did funny things to the sound of their footsteps. Somewhere far out at sea, thunder rumbled. The air became cooler and the puffs of wind were fast becoming gusts.

"I hope your tent stakes are tight," joked Dad to the McGills.

"If they're not," joked Mr. McGill back, "Paul will be grounded for a decade or two."

Back at the campsites, in a wind now blowing hard, everyone scrambled into their tents. That was when Davis started to think about what seemed to him perfectly obvious. *Mooncussers had returned to Cape Cod.* The flashing light from the wrong direction . . . the hoof prints on the beach . . . and finally, the awful coincidence of Mom's story. They all began to weigh heavily on Davis' mind as the first drops of rain pattered gently on the taut roof of their tent.

Davis is synthesizing the events of the day. He is recalling the pieces of information and organizing them to form his idea of what is happening.

As the patter turned to something more like a continuous drumroll, Davis moved restlessly in his sleeping bag.

"What're you doing?" moaned Liz. "Running a marathon? Go to sleep . . . ."

Davis lay motionless, but that made things even worse. His mind filled with horsemen brandishing long knives, riding on the very beach where they'd walked that day. Thunder rumbled close by. Finally, after what seemed like a century, he drifted off to sleep.

Later, a loud clap of thunder and a flash of lightning woke him. He sat up as he had the night before. Liz stirred in her sleep, Dad made a snorting noise, and Mom slept on, unmoving. Again, Davis saw a light outside the tent, only this time it was not flashing. In fact, it *seemed* to be coming closer.

It *seemed* to be coming right toward his tent! There was a slow zipping sound as the tent flap was undone, and a raspy whisper said, "Davis, Davis . . ."

"Wait a minute," thought Davis. "I know that voice."

A face appeared, but it was not the weather-beaten, scarred face of a mooncusser. It was the face of Rennie McGill. She was holding a flashlight.

"Davis," she repeated. "Are you up?"

"Yes," he whispered. "What are you doing? Come in out of the rain!"

"Thanks," she whispered gratefully. "I couldn't sleep, but I didn't want to wake anyone in my family. They'd only be annoyed. So I came to see if you were up. I thought you might be."

"I was," replied Davis. "That last bolt of lightning . . . and I was having . . . thoughts."

"About mooncussers?"

"Yes!" he said. "How did you know?"

"Me, too," she answered. "Do you think there really *were* mooncussers? Or *are*?"

"I don't know," Davis said. His right hand felt something in the dark. It was Rennie's hand. Davis took it and held it. They sat there in the dark until Rennie said, "I think I'm feeling sleepy now. See you tomorrow, Davis."

"OK," whispered Davis. "Tomorrow."

Rennie turned the flashlight on and went back to her tent. Davis crawled into his sleeping bag and fell easily back to sleep.

## And as to whether or not there were, or are, mooncussers—well, who can say?

# WRITE A REVIEW

Think about "The Mystery of the Flashing Lights." Did you like the story? Would you recommend it to a friend? Write a short review giving your opinion and explaining why you feel as you do.

# THE STORY WITHIN THE STORY

Reread the description of Mom's eerie story about the mooncussers. Think about the images the story creates for you. Then draw a scene from Mom's story.

# SEARCHING FOR CLUES

Synthesis is about organizing the different pieces of what we read to gain a new meaning. When reading a mystery, the strategy of synthesizing helps you identify and keep track of clues. Go back to the story to find and list Davis' reasons for thinking the mooncussers had returned. As you read, did you interpret the clues the same way Davis did? What was your final conclusion about the mooncussers? Discuss with a partner.

**Collect! Trading CARDS**

**FUN FADS**

Your Pet

MUST HAVE!

DANCE LESSONS

BEEP BEEP

TRADE

Your Pet

*What is a fad?* It's an object or activity that's wildly popular. When something is a fad, just about everyone wants to get involved.

Most fads last for only a short while—from a couple of months up to a year or two. One short-lived fad was a clever businessman's idea of the perfect pet: a rock that came with care instructions. For six months in 1975, these "pets" were a favorite gift.

Another short-lived fad also had to do with pets—electronic ones. Do you remember when it seemed like every kid you knew had a pocket-sized pet beeping and asking for attention? Were you part of that fad?

The form a fad takes can last for years, even though the subject matter may change. Trading cards and stuffed animals are like this. Kids have been collecting and trading them for years. However, the subject matter changes. What trading cards are popular right now? What kind of stuffed animals are a fad? Do you collect either of these items?

Toys aren't the only fads. What's "hot" in music, dance styles, and fashion changes all the time, too. And sometimes things that were fads in the past come back for another round of popularity. Think about tie-dyed shirts and '60s music!

Can you name three or four of today's fads? Are any of them things you collect or do? Which of today's fads are things that might last for a while? Which might be gone in no time?

# Little Bitty Bugs

### by Maureen Mecozzi

> Listen up, young human!
> Just because you have a big brain inside that thick, bony skull doesn't mean you know beetlejuice about the way things work in the world. Open your eyes a little wider and you'll see who really rules this planet—not people or the biggest of the big. No, it's the teeny, the tiny, the insects—a.k.a.
> **bugs.**

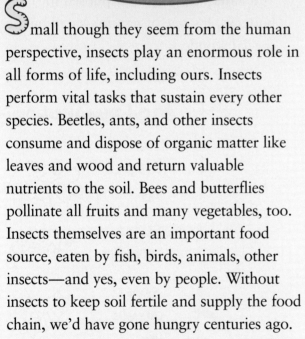

Small though they seem from the human perspective, insects play an enormous role in all forms of life, including ours. Insects perform vital tasks that sustain every other species. Beetles, ants, and other insects consume and dispose of organic matter like leaves and wood and return valuable nutrients to the soil. Bees and butterflies pollinate all fruits and many vegetables, too. Insects themselves are an important food source, eaten by fish, birds, animals, other insects—and yes, even by people. Without insects to keep soil fertile and supply the food chain, we'd have gone hungry centuries ago.

It's time we gave these little creatures the respect they are due. Take a moment to find out more about these seemingly simple animals that are, in fact, the most complex, diverse, and widespread forms of life on Earth.

## Small in Size, Big in Number

About 1 million species of insects have been described to date. But scientists believe there could be many more just waiting to be found and named! Any way you scratch it, that's a LOT of skeeters.

Scientists place the 1 million species of insects into 26 groups. The top five groups are shown in the chart below:

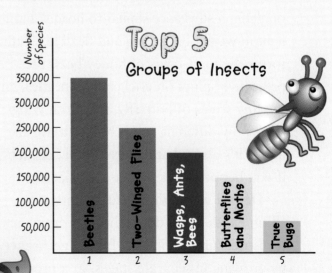

Top 5 Groups of Insects

Number of Species

| | |
|---|---|
| 350,000 | Beetles (1) |
| 300,000 | |
| 250,000 | Two-Winged Flies (2) |
| 200,000 | Wasps, Ants, Bees (3) |
| 150,000 | Butterflies and Moths (4) |
| 100,000 | |
| 50,000 | True Bugs (5) |

**FYI:** The 67,500 species in the fifth group are true bugs, such as bed bugs. These are the only insects that can properly be called *bugs*. An entomologist will tell you that ladybugs and lightning bugs are actually beetles! True bugs have certain characteristics, like mouths that can pierce and suck, that make them different from the other insect orders.

Look back at the chart. How does it convey a lot of information?

**The skeleton of this bug is on the outside, and is called an *exoskeleton*.**

## Tiny but Tough

If there are so many different kinds of insects, why is it that none of them have ever gotten any bigger than a baseball? Even the Goliath beetle, one of the biggest insects, measures only about 4 inches, or 10 centimeters.

It's a simple matter of biology. You have an internal framework of bones called a *skeleton* that supports your organs, muscles, and skin. Insects have a skeleton, too—but theirs is on the *outside*, not the inside, of the body.

An insect's exoskeleton (*exo* means "outside of" in Greek) isn't made of bone, but of *chitin*, a substance similar to horn. Chitin is light in weight but strong and flexible. Chitin forms the furry coats of honey bees, the protective spines on crickets and beetles, and the tiny scales of butterfly and moth wings that show different colors and patterns in light. (It's also what makes a loud "crunch" if you happen to step on a cockroach.)

Despite all its wonderful qualities, a chitin exoskeleton does have one drawback: It restricts growth in size. Insects get bigger by growing in separate stages, in a process

called *metamorphosis*. Several times during the stages of metamorphosis, an insect will grow a new exoskeleton and then molt, or shed, the old one. Perhaps you have watched as a caterpillar metamorphosed into a butterfly. It's one of nature's small but very special wonders.

# Metamorphosis

Stage 1:
egg

Stage 2:
caterpillar

Stage 3:
chrysalis

Stage 4:
butterfly

# What a Short Life!

Compared to humans, most insects don't live very long. A housefly, for instance, can go through an entire life cycle in just 17 days. Mayfly nymphs spend a year living underwater, but once they become adults, life lasts for less than a day. In the late afternoon, the adults emerge, molt twice, mate, and lay eggs in water. Because the adults do not have developed mouth parts, they do not feed, and they die before dawn.

Some locusts live 15 long, dark years underground as grubs. Once they poke their heads above the soil as adults, they have only a few weeks of life left.

Fleas complete their life cycle in two weeks to two years. It depends on the weather and how much food is available. The flea eggs hatch in one to 12 days. The larva stays away from light and feeds for a week or two, then spins a tiny cocoon. The pupa stays in the cocoon from five days to five weeks. When the pupa feels vibrations—for instance, when a dog walks by—it knows a host (and a meal) is near. It emerges from the cocoon, and the adult flea begins looking for the nearest dog or cat to call home!

A favorite of greenhouse operators, the minute pirate bug lives for just three to four weeks. In that short time, though, the little pirates munch on thousands of mites, aphids, and thrips that weaken plants. Spined soldier bugs (also called "stinkbugs") live for three months—long enough to do battle with hornworms,

Here lies poor Jonny Flea. He would have lived a full 22 days, but a shoe got him in just 3!

cabbage loopers, Colorado potato beetles, and other farm pests.

Royalty in the insect world tend to live longer than the average bug. A queen bee can reign for six years, but a worker bee lives for six months—and a drone, just eight weeks, if he's lucky!

How does the subhead at the top of this page summarize this section of the article?

**The "stinkbug" gets its name because of a foul-smelling substance it uses to kill its prey.**

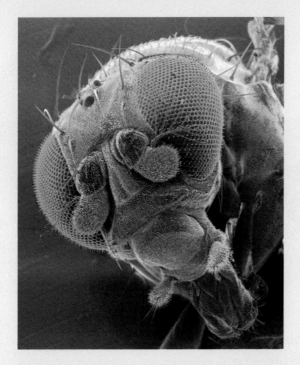

**The large green areas on the head of this fly are its compound eyes. Each eye has about 4,000 facets.**

## Short but Sense-sational

An insect's life may be brief, but it is packed with many more impressions of sight, sound, and smell than a human could experience in the same amount of time.

Insects see with amazing compound eyes. Compound eyes are made up of thousands of *facets*, or simple eyes. The more simple eyes an insect has, the greater its range of vision. Dragonflies, with 30,000 simple eyes, can see objects *behind* them! Compound eyes allow insects to detect movement with great accuracy. That's why it's so hard to swat a fly—it sees you coming the instant you begin to move.

Imagine if you could smell, touch, and hear . . . all with your nose! Insects have just such a multipurpose organ: the antennas. The sense of smell in all insects is located in

Look at the photo of the eyes of a fly above. Read the caption. How do the photo and caption help you understand the text?

their antennas. When one ant finds food, it uses the tip of its abdomen to mark a scented dotted line as it returns to the nest. The other ants follow the spots of scent to the food.

You've probably seen two ants tapping their antennas together, using a deliberate rhythm almost like an insect Morse code. They're exchanging information on food sources, or sending an ant SOS.

Insects living in groups, like honey bees, use smells to communicate. When trouble is near, they release an alarm scent to warn other members of the hive; when the danger is gone, they release a calming, all-clear scent. Bees also use scent as passwords. Only bees that have the proper odor are allowed into the hive.

Insect antennas detect heat, much to the distress of warm-blooded animals like humans. That's why mosquitoes can find you in total darkness. Antennas can also hear certain sounds. When a male mosquito's antennas pick up an F-sharp sound, a female mosquito is certain to be in the area.

"Do you ever get the feeling you're being watched?"

## They're Everywhere

When you know a piece of land the size of a soccer field might contain as many as 5 billion individual insects, perhaps you can get a better picture of just how many insects there are crawling around on any given day. Young human, you're outnumbered!

Insects can survive just about anywhere. Snow fleas in arctic climates stay frisky even at temperatures close to freezing. The larvae of ephyrid flies bask in the waters of hot springs at a steamy 140 degrees F. Desert termites nest 131 feet below ground; African termites build nests 42 feet high above ground. And mosquitoes, the hardiest of all, live quite comfortably both at the frozen Arctic Circle and the sweltering equator. In short, there is no corner of the planet that insects have not conquered.

JEFFERSON ELEMENTARY SOCCER FIELD
Population:
5,000,000,000

Many people fear insects, but most insects help rather than harm us. With nothing more than a pair of sharp eyes, you can visit the unique world of insects. The next time a few ants cross your path, stop for a moment and watch. You'll be observing an entire society in action, just like your own. ◯

**Ladybugs make a kind of antifreeze so they can hibernate in snow.**

# Stop and Respond

## Looking Back

Look at the article again. How do the subheads help you know what each section of the article will be about? Make a list of details from the article that are important to you. Make another list of other things you know about insects. Compare these two lists to help you synthesize the information about insects.

## A Bug's Time Line

Reread the "What a Short Life!" section of the article. Then create an illustrated time line that shows what you learned about one bug's short life span.

Day 1

## Good and Bad

Think about your feelings and reactions toward insects as you read this article. Did you end up feeling positive or negative about bugs? Then make a chart to identify good and bad things about these tiny creatures.

Day 3

| Good Stuff About Bugs | Bad Stuff About Bugs |
|---|---|
| | |

Day 8

# JUST FOR LAUGHS

When you're in a hurry, what kind of math is easiest to do?

short division

Why did the waiter cut the top off the loaf of bread?

A customer had asked for shortbread.

Why did the baseball player want to know how tall he was?

He wanted to know if he was short enough to play shortstop.

When are *a, e, i, o,* and *u* smaller than the other letters in the alphabet?

when they're short vowels

By now, you're probably tired of the word *short!* Here are some synonyms to use instead.

**Words that mean *short in height*:**

| | |
|---|---|
| diminutive | petite |
| elfin | pint-sized |
| little | small |
| miniature | tiny |
| minuscule | wee |

**Words that mean *short in time*:**

| | |
|---|---|
| abbreviated | fleeting |
| brief | momentary |
| compressed | passing |
| concise | perishable |
| condensed | succinct |

# Something to Think About

## SYNTHESIZING

# The Short of It

Keisha's teacher asked her to read the first two articles in this issue and tell her why it is called "Short Stuff." She read "The Mystery of the Flashing Lights" and thought about the characters, the setting, and the plot, and wrote some notes. Then she read "Little Bitty Bugs" and looked at the title, the heads, the facts, and the photographs, and made some notes. Here are her note cards:

## The Mystery of the Flashing Lights

- Davis sees short flashing lights.
- The friends camp together one short week each year.
- The tracks in the sand go a short distance.
- Mom tells a short story about mooncussers.

## Little Bitty Bugs

- Insects are very small.
- There are many kinds of insects all over the world.
- Insects don't live very long.
- These tiny creatures have different senses than people do.

As she reads over her note cards, Keisha **synthesizes** her notes. She considers the individual pieces of information and begins to see two patterns emerge. She realizes that the stories feature different meanings of the word *short*. One is a mystery about short flashing lights, and the other describes very small, or short, insects that live short lives.

Now Keisha wonders how the next two articles will connect to the theme, "Short Stuff." Will they describe things that are short in time or short in height?

# Shoot for the Moon

## by Marilee Robin Burton

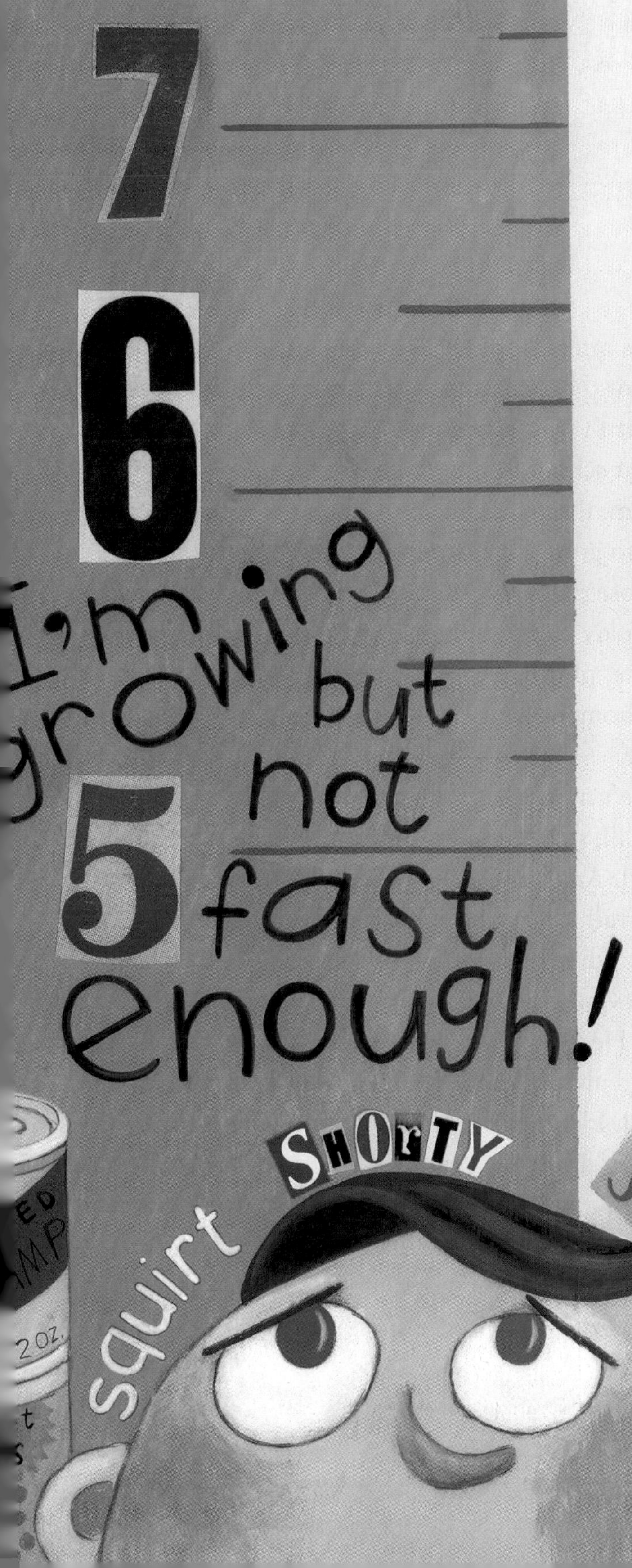

7

6

I'm growing but not fast enough!

5

squirt SHORTY SHRIMP

I've been a short kid my whole life. I know everyone starts off short. But then they grow! Well, I'm growing too, of course. Dad pencils my height on the pantry wall once a month to show it. Yes, I'm growing . . . but not fast enough! I mean, after all, I come from a tall family. Dad's tall. Mom's tall. Sheila's tall. I'm the only one who's still short. Well, that is, except for Uncle Harry. That's Mom's brother. He's a space scientist. He's very smart, very cool, works for NASA, and he's short. Me too. Short. I hope I don't take after Uncle Harry! But I'm the shortest kid in my family. I'm the shortest kid in my class. I'm the shortest kid on the block. Shorty. Shrimp. Squirt.

I'm tired of being short. Mom says I won't always be so short. Dad says that everyone in our family was short before they got tall. Sheila says some day I'll have a growth spurt just like she did. But I say, "What if I take after Uncle Harry?" Uncle Harry always tells Sheila and me to work hard and reach for the moon! Only I figure you have to be tall to reach high. And I want to be tall ASAP. Yes, growing tall is what I want most. Or at least that's what I wanted most until last Friday. That's the day my perspective on short changed.

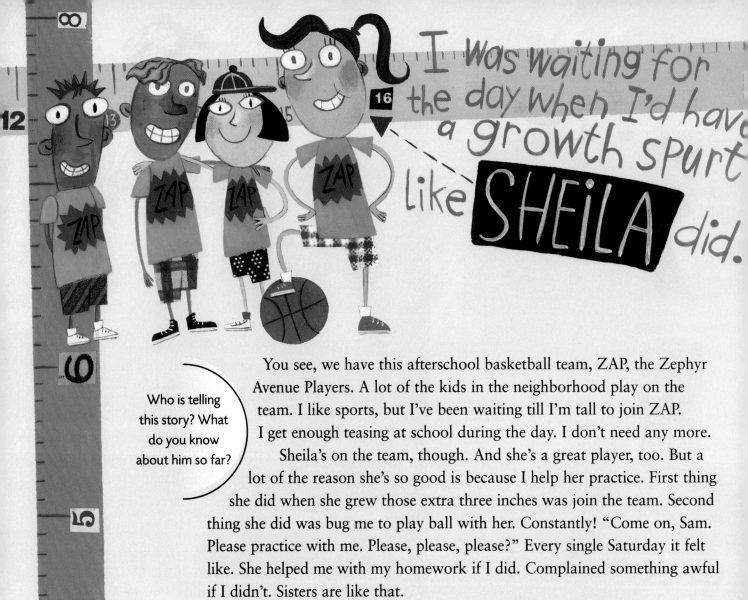

I was waiting for the day when I'd have a growth spurt like SHEILA did.

**Who is telling this story? What do you know about him so far?**

You see, we have this afterschool basketball team, ZAP, the Zephyr Avenue Players. A lot of the kids in the neighborhood play on the team. I like sports, but I've been waiting till I'm tall to join ZAP. I get enough teasing at school during the day. I don't need any more.

Sheila's on the team, though. And she's a great player, too. But a lot of the reason she's so good is because I help her practice. First thing she did when she grew those extra three inches was join the team. Second thing she did was bug me to play ball with her. Constantly! "Come on, Sam. Please practice with me. Please, please, please?" Every single Saturday it felt like. She helped me with my homework if I did. Complained something awful if I didn't. Sisters are like that.

But to tell the truth, I didn't mind practicing hoops with her. That way I'd be ready to play when I got tall, too. I was waiting for the day when I'd have a growth spurt like Sheila did. And as soon as I did, I'd join ZAP, too. No more short kid stuff for me. Tall kid. Tall kid sports. Good to be prepared. If other kids teased me about what I was doing I just said, "MYOB."

So Sheila and I practiced every weekend. Once, Uncle Harry even came to the park and played with us. He was pretty good, too. He clued me in on his secret — "Know your stuff and always shoot for the moon."

So I read up on basketball. I learned everything I could about the sport — about offense, defense, shooting, dribbling, passing. Usually Sheila's the one who bosses me around. She's bigger, and older. But tall or short, I knew basketball.

"Concentrate when you shoot!" I told Sheila. "Keep your eye on the ball," I reminded her. "Always know what's going on all around you," I instructed. I made her work hard for her baskets. I held my hands up when she was trying to shoot. I got good at stealing the ball. And I was fast when I got it. I kept my head up when I dribbled. I used both hands, my elbows close to my body, pushing the ball with my fingers. I balanced. I counterbalanced.

It's true, Sheila's my sister and I wanted to help her be a better player. But I was also discovering that I loved the game. And boy, when I got tall, did I want to be good already! But even before that day, I wanted to be my best and play a good game. Basketball is a cool sport.

Meantime I started asking Dad to measure me once a week instead of once a month. I was thinking about reaching for the moon like Uncle Harry said. And the taller I got, the easier the reach would be. So I wanted to keep checking on that growth spurt. And I *was* growing. Just not three inches at a time. Not yet. Dad measured an eighth of an inch one week. A sixteenth of an inch the next. Well, at least it was something. I was on the slow road to tall.

But right about then a funny thing happened. Sheila and I kept practicing hoops. Sheila for now, me for later. Sheila was getting to be a better and better basketball player *now.* No doubt about it. I knew it. She knew it. And pretty soon the other kids knew it, too. "Practice, practice, practice," Coach Nuefeld had told her. She was. And it was showing. But I was practicing, too.

Before very long, one by one, team kids started coming over to the park on Saturdays. Even Jerold and Hakeem *asked* if they could play. Hakeem and Jerold are co-captains of the team. I guess they could see I was going to be pretty good *later* on, because they asked to play with both of us. Nobody said anything about me sitting out, or watching. Maybe it was those extra eighths

What is happening to Sam and Sheila in the story? How do you predict it will end?

Hey, can I join in?

of an inch, but I don't think so. I was getting to be good *now,* too. Hakeem still called me "Shorty." Sue Anne still asked, "When are you going to grow, Sam?" But they all wanted me in the game, just the same.

Then last Friday I went to another one of the ZAP games. I went to watch, as I always do. You can sure learn a thing or two watching people play.

"Hey Shrimp, how you doing?" Jerold called out the minute he saw me.

"Oh look! The little short kid's here!" Hakeem yelled.

Short. Little. Shrimp. When would things change? But before I could think anymore about that, my sister Sheila threw a true blue perfect pass to me — exactly the way I taught her. Good student! When I caught the ball, she smiled and turned to Coach Nuefeld proudly. "That's my little brother. He taught me everything I know. *He knows basketball!*" A light went on inside my head! I thought of Uncle Harry. *He knows outer space!* He worked hard to become a scientist. He's loves what he does. And he's good at it.

Just then, Hakeem yelled, "Come on, Squirt! Get on the court and start dribbling. We need you on our team!"

Sue Anne shouted, "Come on, Short Stuff, let's go!"

That's the moment I realized *short* is just a word and *tall* is something you feel inside. Before that, I thought I couldn't stand tall unless I grew inches. But suddenly I knew that's not how you measure the tall that counts the most. Uncle Harry was right. Always aim high. But aiming high has nothing to do with height! You know, I might just be proud to take after my Uncle Harry!

Carrying the ball firmly, I strode onto the court. Short or tall, I was ready to reach for the moon. ZAP — here I am! ○

# I was ready to reach for the moon...

# Stop and Respond

## Thinking About the Theme

Review the story, thinking about the issue's theme, "Short Stuff." Write a sentence that explains how "Shoot for the Moon" connects to this theme.

## Story Elements

A good story summary involves synthesizing the important elements and organizing the different pieces to create a meaning greater than the sum of each piece. Create a chart like the one below that identifies the story elements from "Shoot for the Moon." Then write your summary of the story. Did you include information about each element?

## Making Comparisons

Think of a time when you wanted to do something, despite obstacles in your path. Or think of a time when you were afraid to do something because of what others might think. How did you feel? How do these experiences help you understand the feelings of the main character in "Shoot for the Moon"? Discuss with a partner.

| Character | Setting | Sequence of Events | Problem | Resolution |
|-----------|---------|--------------------|---------|------------|
| short boy | Sam's home and neighborhood | | | |

# Miniatures on Parade

**by Linda Johns**

Emperor — 20"

Little — 10"

**C**an you think of anything that could make a penguin cuter? What if the penguin was so little that you could hold it in your hand? What if you saw dozens of these tiny tuxedos waddling across the beach in a penguin parade? That kind of "penguins on parade" is exactly what visitors to Phillip Island in southwestern Australia can see nearly every night of the year.

Little penguins are flightless birds, just like emperor, humboldt, and all 17 species of penguins. Once called *fairy penguins,* they are now officially known as *little penguins,* which is exactly what they are. A full-grown little penguin weighs two pounds and stands about ten inches tall—about half the height of an emperor penguin.

The unofficial "Penguin Parade" starts at sunset on Phillip Island. First one or two come waddling out of the water and onto the beach. A few more follow. Soon a dozen more little penguins come along. They march, stumble, and tumble along the shore as they head for their bedtime nests.

Hundreds of tourists watch the penguins each night. Hundreds of penguins take part each night. Some nights there may be 200 penguins; other times there may be 800 or 900. People can watch, but they cannot get too close. These birds are protected in their natural habitat.

So what is it that makes this spectacle so endearing? Penguins are always entertaining to watch. But there's something extra here. It's the same appeal all kinds of miniature animals have. We're fascinated by small versions of things that seem familiar to us.

## GOING FOR A RIDE

Quick. Think of a pint-sized version of a farm animal. Quite possibly you thought of a pony. Maybe you're even remembering your first pony ride when you were little. Maybe the pony seemed gigantic to you back then!

You already know that *pony* isn't just another word for a young horse. A pony is a special breed of horse that stays small, even when full-grown. Any horse smaller than 58 inches high is officially called a pony. (The height of a horse or a pony is measured from the ground to the top of its shoulders.)

Shetland ponies first came from the Shetland Islands in Scotland, where they were used as pack horses. The small horses were used to working in harsh conditions and with little food. Some people in England used them to work in the coal mines. Ponies arrived in the U.S. in about 1850, and were bred to be pets. A Shetland pony's gentle manner and small size makes it ideal for giving children rides!

There are other kinds of ponies, too, such as Welsh ponies. But the Shetland is the smallest breed of horse, usually reaching only about 40 inches high.

## SMALLER THAN A YARDSTICK

If a Shetland pony is the smallest horse in the world, what's up with those miniature horses some people raise? Are they fake?

Actually, a Shetland is the smallest naturally occurring horse. That doesn't mean miniature horses (called *minis*) are unnatural. Somewhere in the past, some horses had a genetic mutation that led them to be born unusually small. People then bred these small horses on purpose. Now you can find miniature horses in all different colors and breeds, including palominos, pintos, and chestnuts.

The American Mini-Horse Association (AMHA) registers minis that are 34 inches or under. Get a ruler and mark off 34 inches. Now compare that to the 60 inches or taller a full-sized horse is! Minis are perfectly proportioned small horses. That means they have all the same parts and traits as full-sized horses. They also have all the same needs. Minis need food, water, shelter, grooming, and attention from their human owners.

> How does the subhead at the top of this column relate to the information in this paragraph?

# WE'RE NOT KIDDING!

Some farmers who raise goats might have some really little kids mixed in with their herd. No, not human kids! We're talking about baby goats, which are called *kids*. These wobbly four-legged creatures are always cute, but a Nigerian dwarf goat's tiny kids are as small as puppies.

Nigerian dwarf goats originally came from West Africa. They can be black and white, brown, brown and white, or a gold color. Even with all four feet on the ground, these dairy goats are less than two feet tall. A full-grown male, called a *buck*, might be around 23 inches.

Common — 36"

Nigerian — 23"

# WHAT A DEAR LITTLE DEER!

In 1997, Alan Rabinowitz, a biologist for the Wildlife Conservation Society (WCS), spotted a tiny deer in Burma in Southeast Asia. The adult deer was just 20 inches tall at the shoulder and weighed less than 25 pounds. Rabinowitz brought one back to New York where scientists did DNA analysis.

The DNA testing confirmed that the *leaf muntjac,* or leaf deer, is a new species of deer. The leaf deer is also the smallest kind of deer known.

Was this deer so shy that it went unnoticed? Or was it so small that it didn't catch the human eye? Actually, the leaf deer lives in a very remote mountain area in Southeast Asia. Not many people live there. People native to the area had spotted the small deer before, but scientists had not. In the past ten years, biologists and researchers have been spending more time in Southeast Asia studying animals. New species of large mammals have been found, too.

How do the leaves in the photo help you understand how tiny the deer is?

# small names

The words *dwarf* and *pygmy* are often used in the official name of small animals to let you know right away that this is an unusually small version of another animal. Some huge animals have smaller relatives that still seem pretty big. For instance, the sperm whale has both a dwarf version and a pygmy version. For years scientists lumped the two smaller versions together. The pygmy sperm whale is about 10 to 11 feet long. Sure, that sounds big—and it's at least twice as long as you are! But compare that pygmy sperm whale to a 60-foot sperm whale, and you can see why scientists use the word *pygmy!*

The dwarf sperm whale is even smaller than its pygmy cousin. It usually measures between eight and nine feet long. It has a rounder head than the pygmy sperm whale. It probably hunts and lives deeper in the ocean than the pygmy sperm whale. Guess how scientists know that? The best clue is to see what the whales have eaten! The dwarf sperm whale's stomach tends to have food in it from 250 feet down in the ocean.

How do the scale diagrams help you understand the size of the animals?

Common — 5'
Pygmy — 3'

Even a hippopotamus can be tiny—at least compared to a regular hippopotamus. The pygmy hippopotamus lives on the west coast of Africa. It's about two-and-a-half to three feet tall. Compare that to hippos you've seen at the zoo!

The pygmy hippo looks quite a lot like a pig. In fact, it's now known that all hippos are more closely related to pigs than to horses. But their name comes from Greek, and means "river horse."

## Get Along, Little Doggie

What did the cowboy say to the dachshund? You got it: "Get along, little doggie!" When you think of a long, little dog, you probably think of a dachshund. These adorable short-legged dogs are the target of many jokes about hot dogs and wiener dogs. A dachshund is pretty good-natured, so it may even laugh along with you—especially if you've got a doggie treat to share.

Dachshunds have strong muscles and stand proud for such short little canines. They're usually about 12 to 14 inches tall. A toy version can be less than 12 inches tall and weigh only six to eight pounds. Not surprisingly, these long bodies can have back problems. Watch a dachshund run and you can see why: Its short legs move fast and its body has to wiggle to keep up.

Of course, there is a dog even smaller than a dachshund. Can you guess what it is? Yep—it's a Chihuahua, the smallest dog alive. It reaches a towering five inches and weighs less than two pounds. This makes the Chihuahua the ultimate lap dog. How did it get this unusual name? The Chihuahua originally came from the state of Chihuahua in Mexico.

> How much shorter is a Chihuahua than a dachshund?

Excitement over discovering the leaf deer and other species influences people to protect the environment. People are realizing that there are more kinds of animals co-existing on this planet than they believed and that these animals need protection. There is one thing all these tiny treasures have in common. From a five-inch Chihuahua to a six-foot pygmy whale, each living thing deserves the right environment in which to thrive. Growing up small is just as important as growing up tall.  ◎

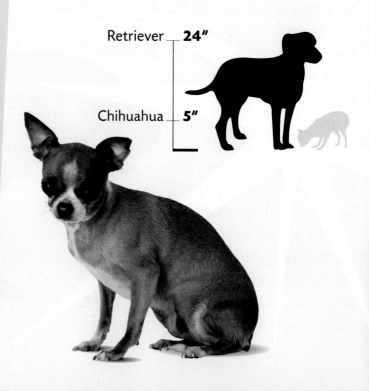

Retriever — 24"

Chihuahua — 5"

# COMPARISON DRAWING

Use what you learned from the article to make a comparison drawing. Choose one of the animals that has a miniature and a full-size version, such as penguins, horses, goats, deer, whales, and hippos. Reread the section on that animal and look for details about size. Use that information to create a drawing that compares the miniature and full-size versions of these animals.

# SEEING PATTERNS

Synthesizing is the process of collecting a large assortment of facts and sorting them into groups with a common theme or idea. One skill that makes it easier to synthesize what you need is the ability to see patterns. A helpful pattern often found in nonfiction is the use of subheads. Go through the story again. List each of the subheads in the article. Then choose three subheads and summarize each of the sections in one or two sentences.

# SHORT AND TALL

From reading the article, you know that "short" is relative. After all, at 10 feet long, a pygmy sperm whale is only short when compared to a normal sperm whale! Have fun thinking of some short and tall pairs. For example, an ape would seem short next to King Kong; an elephant would seem short next to a dinosaur. List five short and tall pairs of your own.

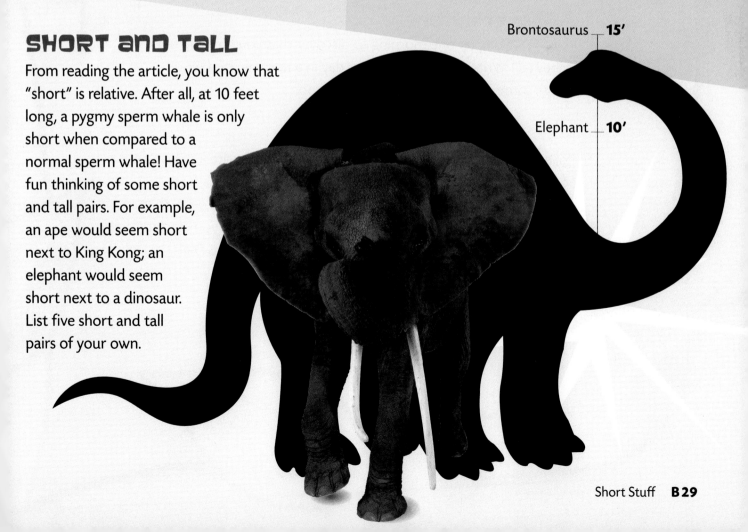

Brontosaurus __ **15'**

Elephant __ **10'**

## Let's Write

## Haiku

One of the shortest forms of poetry is the Japanese haiku. A haiku has only three lines and 17 syllables. Its theme usually has something to do with nature.

Try creating your own haiku, using the model below. Then illustrate your poem.

| | |
|---|---|
| *Title* ⟶ | **Ladybug** |
| *Line 1 (5 syllables)* ⟶ | Sitting on a leaf; |
| *Line 2 (7 syllables)* ⟶ | wings unfold, ready to fly |
| *Line 3 (5 syllables)* ⟶ | on the rising wind. |

## A Short Nightmare

Imagine waking up one morning to discover that you are only ten inches tall! Write a story about your day in a normal-sized world. Create some illustrations for your story, too.

## Make a Mini-Book

Collect records and trivia about short things. Then create a miniature book to share the results of your research. Make the pages from paper cut into three-inch squares. Write one fact on each page, then staple pages together in book form. Here's a fact to get you started: The shortest complete sentence in the English language is *I am.*

## More Books

Levine, Shar; Humphrey, Elaine; & Johnstone, Leslie. *3-D Bees and Micro Fleas*. Somerville House, 1999.

Norton, Mary. *The Borrowers*. Harcourt, 1998.

Sonenklar, Carol. *Bug Girl*. Yearling, 2000.

White, E.B. *Stuart Little*. Harper, 1999.

Wilcox, Charlotte. *Miniature Horses (Learning About Horses)*. Capstone, 1997.

## On the Web

**Bad Fads Museum**
http://www.badfads.com/home.html

**Tom Thumb**
http://home.wirefire.com/cvance/story/history.htm

**Pygmies**
http://www.mc.maricopa.edu/anthro/exploratorium/diasporas/short.html

**Toy and Miniatures Museum**
http://www.thomes.net/toys

## Across the Curriculum

### Social Studies

Do some research about the shortest people in the world—the Pygmies. How short are they? Where do they live? What do we know about them? Make a poster or write a paragraph to share what you learned.

### Science

Investigate tiny creatures with short lives—insects. Carefully capture an insect that doesn't sting, such as an ant, housefly, or sowbug. Place the insect in a clear container with a lid. Study it with a magnifying glass. Can you identify the insect's antennas, six legs, three body parts, and hard exoskeleton? Then release it outside.

# For Short

People are always looking for ways to shorten things—even words. Here are some of the ways we make words quick and easy to use! Can you think of other examples for each group?

## Portmanteau Words are two words combined to make a new word. The meanings are combined into something new as well!

| | |
|---|---|
| brunch | breakfast + lunch |
| chortle | chuckle + snort |
| clash | clap + crash |
| Eurasia | Europe + Asia |
| flurry | flutter + hurry |
| guesstimate | guess + estimate |
| heliport | helicopter + airport |
| smog | smoke + fog |
| splatter | splash + spatter |

## Acronyms are made up of initials, but pronounced as words.

| | |
|---|---|
| laser | Light amplification by stimulated emission of radiation |
| radar | Radio detecting and ranging |
| RAM | Random access memory |
| scuba | Self-contained underwater breathing apparatus |
| snafu | Situation normal, all fouled up |
| sonar | Sound navigation ranging |
| UNICEF | United Nations International Children's Education Fund |
| WHO | World Health Organization |

## Initializations use initials, but are pronounced by saying the name of each letter.

| | |
|---|---|
| A.K.A. | Also known as |
| ASAP | As soon as possible |
| BLT | Bacon, lettuce, and tomato |
| FYI | For your information |
| MYOB | Mind your own business |
| RV | Recreational vehicle |
| SOS | Save our ship |
| TGIF | Thank goodness it's Friday |
| TLC | Tender loving care |
| VIP | Very important person |

## Abbreviations are a shorter way to write words, but are said as the whole word.

| | | | |
|---|---|---|---|
| Ave. | avenue | ft. | foot |
| ch. | chapter | Jan. | January |
| doz. | dozen | lb. | pound |
| Dr. | doctor | Mr. | Mister |

## Shortened Words are just that—shorter and quicker to say!

| | | | |
|---|---|---|---|
| deli | delicatessen | gym | gymnasium |
| exam | examination | hippo | hippopotamus |
| flu | influenza | rhino | rhinoceros |
| gator | alligator | | |

COMPREHENSION QUARTERLY

CQ 5

ISSUE C: Inferring

# Fooled Again

# Fooled Again

## THINK ABOUT: Inferring

**FICTION**

### Please Come to Dinner; The Monkey, the Mice, and the Cheese

Read these foolish folktales to see who gets tricked.

**C4**

**C11**

**NONFICTION**

### Master of Magic and Mystery

Harry Houdini was known for his amazing magic tricks. Read about his life.

**FICTION**

### The Best Gold

Is a gold medal really the best kind of gold?

**C19**

**C25**

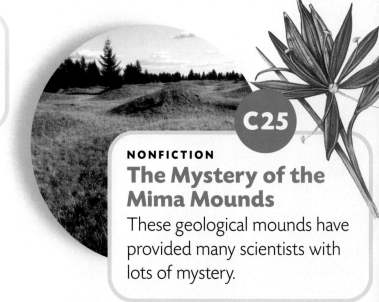

**NONFICTION**

### The Mystery of the Mima Mounds

These geological mounds have provided many scientists with lots of mystery.

## INFERRING

# The Soccer Game

We make predictions every day. For example, we may predict what the weather will be like. How do we make predictions? We use what we observe about a situation (*such as dark rain clouds in the sky*), add what we already know (*that dark rain clouds mean rain*), and then make a prediction (*we'll need our umbrellas today*). As events change, our predictions often change with them.

We predict when we read, too. The stories we read may remind us of similar characters, situations, or our own experiences. We remember the outcomes of other situations and use that knowledge to make **inferences,** or new interpretations, about the story. Unexpected story events can make us rethink our predictions.

Read the paragraph below. Make a three-column chart. On the left, write down what Joel predicted will happen at a soccer game. In the middle, list the information that led Joel to make the prediction. Leave the last column blank.

*Joel had to go to his sister's soccer game, and he dreaded it. The girls were first graders, so they didn't know how to dribble or pass. "How do they expect to score a goal?" he asked his mom. "The games are so boring and there's no one for me to talk to."*

Now read the next paragraph. Which events confirm Joel's prediction? Which events, if any, give him second thoughts? Use the third column in your chart to write the event that either confirms or contradicts Joel's prediction.

*At the field, Joel plopped down on the bleachers. Sure enough, there was not another kid his age in sight. The ref blew the whistle to start the game. Joel let his mind wander, but out of the corner of his eye, he noticed that his sister Beth suddenly broke away from the swarm and dribbled the ball toward the opponent's side. Meanwhile, their goalie was kicking the dirt absent-mindedly. Beth passed the ball to a teammate, who kicked the ball into the goal. "Woo-hooooo!" Josh yelled. Before he knew it, the game was over.*

Joel made a prediction, checked it against new events, and eventually realized that he was wrong. Readers, too, change and check their predictions as they read. Charts, like the three-column one, help readers keep track of these predictions.

# Please Come to Dinner

## An Ashanti Folktale Retold by Angela Shelf Medearis

*The following folktales have more than food in common. After you read them both, see if you can figure out just what it is.*

It was hot! Turtle had been walking for a long time. He hadn't eaten anything since sunrise. Suddenly, Turtle smelled something extraordinary. There was no sign of anyone around. Turtle sniffed the air again. The smell was coming from a house close by. He walked as fast as a turtle can walk, until he came to a small house. His friend, the snake, lived there.

"Hello, hello," Turtle called. "Is anyone at home?"

"Hello," Snake called back. "Please, come in and close the door."

Turtle crawled inside. Snake was stirring a large pot of stew. He was baking some rolls that were so light and fluffy, they spilled over the top of the muffin tin.

"Friend," Turtle said, "may I eat dinner with you? I am very hungry. I haven't had any food since sunrise."

Now, Snake was a very greedy fellow. He hated to share his food. He quickly thought of a trick to keep the stew and rolls all to himself.

"Yes," Snake said, "but first you must wash your hands. It is bad manners to eat without washing your hands first. There is a small pond down the hill. You can wash your hands there."

"Thank you," Turtle said. "I'll be right back."

Turtle crawled down the hill as fast as a turtle can crawl. He washed his hands in the pond. Then he crawled back up the hill.

When he got back to the house, Snake was halfway finished with the stew and most of the rolls.

"Ah, there you are, my brother," Snake said. "I'm sorry, but you took so long, I started dinner without you. Oh my, look at your hands!"

Turtle looked down at his hands in the fading light of day. They were covered with dust.

"Please go wash your hands again," Snake said.

"But I already did," Turtle said.

"Well, you didn't do a very good job," Snake replied. "Go wash your hands again."

Turtle crawled down the hill as fast as a turtle can crawl. Again he washed his hands in the pond. Again he crawled back up the hill.

When he got back to the house, Snake was finished with the meal.

"Ah, there you are, my brother," Snake said. "I'm sorry, but you took so long, I finished dinner without you."

"I see," Turtle said. He was very sad. He knew his friend had played a trick on him.

"Well," Turtle said, "maybe you can eat dinner with me tomorrow."

"I'd love to!" Snake said.

"Just wait by the telephone for my call," said Turtle. "I'll let you know when dinner is ready."

"Wonderful!" Snake answered. "I'll see you tomorrow."

Turtle was a very good cook. Snake dreamed about food all night. He thought about food all day long the next day. The instant the phone rang, Snake answered.

"Please come to dinner," said Turtle. "Everything is ready."

"I'll be right there," said Snake.

Snake was very hungry. He slithered as fast as snakes can to Turtle's house.

Turtle was waiting for Snake by the edge of the river.

"My house is under the water," Turtle said. "Everything is ready. Follow me."

Turtle slipped into the water and swam down to the bottom. Snake tried to follow him. He swam as hard as he could. But he kept floating

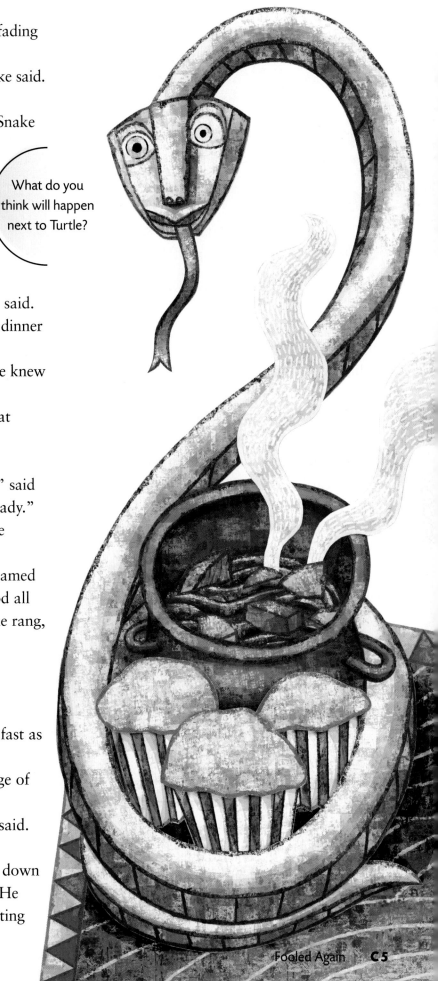

What do you think will happen next to Turtle?

"Oh," Snake said, "I didn't know that." As soon as Snake removed his coat, he floated back to the top of the water.

"Please excuse me, my brother," Turtle called up to Snake. "But under the present circumstances, I'm going to have to eat dessert without you. Please join me when you are ready to eat."

"I'm ready to eat right now!" Snake said. "But I keep floating up to the top." Suddenly, Snake thought of another plan. He climbed out of the water. This time, he put the rocks inside his mouth. He slowly sank down to the bottom of the river.

"There you are, my brother," Turtle said. "I'm sorry, but you took so long, I finished dinner without you."

Snake was very angry. When he opened his mouth to talk, all the rocks fell out. Snake floated back to the top of the water.

"Good-bye," Turtle said. "Thank you for coming to dinner."

"Good-bye," Snake mumbled, as he slithered away.

And Snake never tried to trick Turtle again.

right back up to the top. He was too light to sink to the bottom.

"Please excuse me, my brother," Turtle called up to Snake. "But I am very hungry. I am going to start dinner without you. Please join me when you are ready to eat."

"I'm ready to eat now!" Snake said. "I keep floating up to the top of the water."

"I'm sorry to hear that," Turtle said. "But you must come down here if you want to eat dinner."

Then Snake thought of a plan. He climbed out of the water. He picked up some rocks and put them in his coat pockets. Snake slowly sank down to the bottom of the river.

"Ah, there you are, my brother," Turtle said. "Come and join me. Let me help you remove your coat."

"No, I want to keep it on," Snake said.

"I'm sorry," Turtle said, "but that isn't the right thing to do. It is very bad manners to eat with your coat on."

> What do you think will happen when Snake removes his coat?

> How did your predictions change as you read the story?

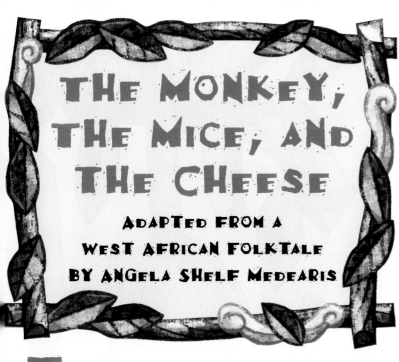

# THE MONKEY, THE MICE, AND THE CHEESE

## ADAPTED FROM A WEST AFRICAN FOLKTALE BY ANGELA SHELF MEDEARIS

Two mice found a large piece of cheese near a tent at a country fair.

"What a trophy!" said the white mouse.

"I knew we'd find a good meal if we looked long enough!" said the brown mouse.

The two little mice transported the cheese across the field by pushing and pulling it. Finally, they reached their mouse hole. They tried to *push* the cheese inside. It wouldn't fit. They tried to *pull* the cheese inside. It wouldn't fit. It was too big to go inside their mouse hole.

"Let's divide the cheese," said the white mouse.

What do you think will happen next?

"Half for you, and half for me," said the brown mouse.

"I'll cut it," said the white mouse.

"No," objected the brown mouse. "I'll cut it."

"This cheese is mine," said the white mouse. "I saw it first."

"No," said the brown mouse. "I saw it first."

A monkey watched the two mice pull the cheese back and forth.

"Stop!" said the monkey. "You shouldn't let your friendship be ruined by such a thing as a piece of cheese! Let me divide it for you."

"That sounds fair," said the white mouse.

The monkey cut the cheese into two pieces.

"Oh no," said the monkey. "One piece is bigger than the other piece." He broke off a bit of the larger piece of cheese and popped it into his mouth.

"Oh no," said the monkey. "Now this piece is smaller than the other."

The monkey bit off some of the other piece of cheese.

"Oh no," said the monkey. "The pieces are still uneven."

The monkey ate bite after bite of the cheese. Soon, there were only two small pieces left.

How do you think this story will end? What makes you think so?

"Stop," said the brown mouse. "You're eating all of our cheese."

"Please give us back our cheese," said the white mouse.

"Give me the big piece," said the brown mouse.

"No," said the white mouse. "Give *me* the big piece."

"No," said the monkey. "I can't give the cheese back to you. If I do, you will start arguing again."

The monkey hung upside down. He swung from limb to limb. "I know what I'll do," said the monkey. He took the rest of the cheese and ate it. "Now you don't have anything to argue about." The monkey laughed and laughed as he swung from branch to branch.

The white mouse and the brown mouse crawled into their hole. And they never argued again. ◯

## THE MORAL OF THE STORY IS . . .

Divide the class into small groups. Assign each group one of the folktales you just read. Let students in each group write down what they think is the moral of the story assigned to them. Read each group's moral out loud, and let the class vote on their favorites.

## A CLASSIC LESSON

Think back to some of the traditional tales that you heard growing up, like *Little Red Riding Hood* or *The Three Little Pigs.* How were the characters fooled in these tales? What lessons did the characters in these stories learn? With a partner, reread one of these traditional tales, and then talk about the foolish actions of the characters and the lessons they learned. You might even want to share these traditional tales with younger students.

## GREED AND FOOLISHNESS

Why is it foolish to be greedy? Often, greedy people lose out in the end—they wind up with lots of stuff but no friends. Think about the two folktales you have just read. Use examples from the stories or from your own experience to write a short poem about what can happen to someone who is greedy.

# Don't Be Fooled by Food!

Your parents always tell you not to play with your food. They might change their thinking if you mention that some people are paid to do just that—play with their food. These lucky people are food stylists, people who prepare food for photography by making it look as good as possible.

But food styling doesn't mean just making volcanoes out of mashed potatoes and gravy or making ice-cream sundaes all day. Food stylists sometimes spend hours, using a variety of tools and finely tuned skills, making the food look so delicious that it makes people want to buy it.

While you may drive your parents crazy twirling pasta around and around on your fork or trying to eat peas with your butter knife, food stylists have a different set of tools to play with. These include eyedroppers, putty knives, cotton swabs, toothbrushes, surgical tweezers, and spray bottles. Each tool has a special purpose. For example, very tiny tweezers are used to move specks of parsley or crumbs.

Food stylists make the food we see on TV and in magazines look delicious. Take a chicken, for example. You see a chicken in an ad that is plump with warm, delicious-looking juices. You can almost smell it as you sit in front of the TV. The TV chicken doesn't look anything like the wrinkled chicken that your mom just took out of the oven after an hour of baking.

So how are they different? For one thing, the TV chicken is raw in the middle. It's been cooked for only 30 minutes, so it's still plump and juicy. Because the chicken hasn't cooked long enough to brown, the stylist paints it with a sauce that is a mixture of dishwashing soap and other ingredients to make a brown color. The soap makes the sauce stick to the fat of the skin. Sounds delicious, huh?

Because ice cream would melt under the hot lights in a TV studio, many food stylists use mashed potatoes instead. Others use a special recipe of solid vegetable shortening, confectioner's sugar, and corn syrup that has been mixed together. Try that with chocolate syrup!

So the next time the food on TV makes your mouth water, think about why it looks so good—it's probably been painted, glued, pinned, or picked at by a professional food stylist.

# Master of *Magic* and **Mystery**

*by David R. Collins*

*A* cold winter breeze swept over the frozen Detroit River. Several hundred spectators gathered to watch a man climb to the top of the bridge and look downward. Below lay the outline of a hole in the ice that was just big enough to fit a man through. Several eager newspaper reporters tried to push forward, but a human wall of policemen held firm. The crowd watched silently as the man on the bridge raised his arms to display a pair of gleaming handcuffs on his wrists. His slender body, dressed only in a pair of plain white trunks, shivered briefly and then went streaking downward. Several screams broke the silence of the crowd as he splashed into the icy water.

"Why, the mere shock would kill a normal person," gasped a Detroit doctor.

"Yeah, but who says Houdini's normal?" replied a young man standing nearby.

Beneath the surface of the water, Harry Houdini struggled to get the pair of handcuffs from his wrists. In a matter of seconds, the handcuffs were unlocked, and he eagerly pushed upward. He was pleased with how quickly he had freed himself, but now he was anxious to find freedom from the cold water.

Suddenly his head cracked against the hard ice. For a moment, he was stunned. He realized now that his battle for survival was just beginning—he had lost the opening in the ice! He did not know how far the river's current had brought him, but he knew he had to find the opening fast!

A silence had fallen over the crowd above. Two minutes had passed since Houdini had disappeared from sight, and a few worried faces began to appear.

**Above:** A group of men watch magician Harry Houdini get into a crate as part of a performance of one of his infamous escape tricks.

# "How did you do it?"

"He didn't take this long in New York City when I saw him," murmured a woman.

"Perhaps the cold slows him down a little," whispered her husband.

After another minute or two had passed with still no sign of him, a diver prepared to enter the water. He fastened a rope to the bridge and dropped it into the open hole below.

One reporter quickly sensed concern among Houdini's team. Running to the closest phone, he broke the worried silence with cries of "Houdini's dead! They're going in after him!"

Then, as Houdini's assistant was climbing down the rope, two hands and a bobbing head suddenly appeared at the surface. A joyous howling spread across the rows of spectators—Houdini had done it again!

*What do you think is going to happen to Houdini?*

Climbing out of the water, Houdini shook violently as he slid into the warmth of a heavy coat. He threw his arms around two of his friends as the spectators crowded around for a closer look at the man who cheated death for a living.

"How did you do it?" asked an enthusiastic reporter. "You were down for eight minutes!"

"Well, it wasn't *so* difficult," answered Houdini. "The handcuffs weren't any challenge, but I had lost the opening when I was ready to come up. I had to float near the surface and use the air between the ice and water to breathe. I'd gulp some air and then submerge to look for the light from the opening. Scraped my nose on the ice a few times, but I guess I can't complain."

"But weren't you frightened?" another reporter asked, amazed.

"Well, I guess I was for a little while— maybe about eight minutes' worth!" Houdini winked and walked away.

Who was this man that thrilled millions of people all over the world with his amazing, daring feats?

Harry Houdini was born Ehrich Weiss in 1874. As a child in Appleton, Wisconsin, he spent much of his time mastering magic tricks. When he wasn't showing his tricks to neighborhood friends, he was developing demanding exercises to give himself control over the muscles of his body.

At the age of twelve, Ehrich left home and roamed the Midwest, finding odd jobs to support himself. As a locksmith's assistant, he became fascinated with locks and carefully studied their secrets. He soon found he could pick any lock using a 2-inch piece of wire.

When he was fifteen, Ehrich started performing in public. Though he followed the usual routine of card tricks, rabbits in silk hats, and disappearing eggs, his swiftness and muscle coordination dazzled his audiences.

As he was performing his act one night at a country fair, one of the spectators made the statement that all magicians were the same.

"You're just another fake," the man yelled. "You'd better grow up and learn a few good tricks."

Ehrich was furious. He was proud of his act, and the insult hurt him deeply. Then he spotted the county sheriff standing nearby.

"Say, Sheriff, do you suppose I can borrow your handcuffs for a minute or two?"

The sheriff, realizing how complicated handcuffs are, hesitated.

"Please, Sheriff. It will just take a minute, and I promise to return them or give you money for *two* pairs."

Immediately, the crowd began to urge the sheriff to loan the young magician the handcuffs. He finally walked forward and gave them to Ehrich.

"No, Sheriff, just lock them on," Ehrich said loudly.

The sheriff, looking doubtful, locked the handcuffs on and stepped backward, holding the key high in the air so that the crowd could easily see it. Ehrich quickly slipped behind a screen on the small stage. Seconds later, he emerged with the handcuffs dangling from his right wrist.

Will Ehrich get out of the handcuffs or not? Why do you think that?

"How in the world . . . " gasped the sheriff. "I just received these cuffs this morning from Washington, and I know you couldn't have a key."

**Above:** Some of Houdini's most famous stunts used chains and padlocks. Later, he would be known as "The Handcuff King."

# Stop and Respond

## Book Magic

When Houdini died, he left behind an amazing library of books about magic. Use the library or your computer to find books about this subject, whether they are about Houdini and other famous magicians or about how to perform magic tricks. Put together your own bibliography of books that you would like to read. Then read them!

## Come One and All!

Research some of the tricks that made Houdini famous. Use the information you find to create a poster inviting people to see one of Houdini's shows. On your poster, include quotations about the great magician and an exciting picture of Houdini performing one of his famous tricks.

## Eyewitness to History

Imagine that you are a news reporter covering one of Houdini's stunning feats. Gather information from books, magazine articles, and the Internet. Use the information to write a news article that answers the five *W*'s of journalism: *who, what, when, where,* and *why.*

It's a sunny day. All day you've looked forward to gym class, when you could go outside for a game of dodgeball. However, when you get to gym class, the teacher is holding a stack of papers. "Class," he says seriously, "today I'm giving you a quiz about all of the games we've learned so far." So much for the sunshine! His voice is all but drowned out by the groans of 25 fifth graders, when the teacher yells, "April Fools!"

Have you ever played an April Fool's Day joke on someone? Maybe you've changed your sister's clock so she thinks she's late for swim practice. Or you told someone that you won one hundred dollars. Maybe you've even been the victim of an April Fool's joke. Perhaps you've found an "I'm a fool!" sign taped to your back. If anything like this has ever happened to you, you're just part of the practical jokes played on April Fool's Day.

Although Americans have celebrated April Fool's Day since colonial times, it is not just an American holiday. In France, the holiday is called "April Fish." In a prank much like the famous "sign on the back," the French tape a paper fish to their friends' backs. When onlookers discover the fish, they yell *Poisson d'Avril!* (April Fish!) In England, if a trick is played on you, you are called a "noodle." In Scotland, April Fool's Day is 48 hours long and a prank victim is called "April Gowk," or "cuckoo bird." The traditional April Fool's Day trick in Portugal is to throw flour at your friends.

No one knows exactly when the April Fool's Day custom started. Some historians say that April Fool's Day began as a celebration of spring. People celebrated by playing pranks on each other. Others argue that April Fool's Day started around 1564, when the new calendar was adopted in France. During the Middle Ages, the new year had begun on March 25. People celebrated with eight days of parties that ended on April 1.

As part of the calendar change, however, King Charles IX moved New Year's Day from April 1 to January 1. Many people, whether because they hadn't heard the news or because they didn't like change, kept celebrating New Year's on April 1. Such people were labeled "fools" and became the victims of such pranks as fake party invitations and gag gifts. And the rest is history.

# Something to Think About

## INFERRING

## I Predict . . .

As we read a book, we make predictions. These predictions are often based on what we've read so far in the book and whatever background knowledge we bring to the book as we read. Predictions are a part of **inferring.**

As a reader, you make predictions all the time, probably without even realizing it. When you pick a book up and look at the cover, you predict what the book will be about by reading the title, checking out the author's name, and by looking at the cover illustration. When you decide that the book looks interesting, you are making a prediction that it will be a book you might enjoy reading.

As you begin reading, you may change your mind about the book. Perhaps you thought it was going to be a funny book, but it turns out to be more serious than you had hoped. As you continue reading, you continue to make predictions about what will happen. You base your predictions on what has happened so far in the story, and also on your background knowledge. Perhaps you have been in a similar situation as the main character. You can make a prediction about what will happen because you've been in that same situation.

As we make and revise our predictions as we read, we are creating our own personal interpretations of the book. As you read "The Best Gold," think about the predictions you make along the way. How will your own experiences help you to make predictions? Be thinking about whether your predictions turn out to be correct or whether you revise your predictions along the way.

# The Best Gold

by Claire Daniel

Lights flashed from cameras, and reporters pushed one another to get a look at the familiar face of the Olympic gold medal winner. The twenty-year-old swimmer was a five-time champion, but she was tired and anxious to relax after an exhausting week at the Olympics.

"Miss Perella, may I have an interview, please?" one reporter yelled above the crowd.

Kim Perella looked at the young man and said, "If you can keep it short, you can have the interview."

The reporter agreed and followed the swimmer and her coach to a quiet room off the lobby of the hotel. They sat down in comfortable chairs, and Kim asked the reporter, "OK, so what do you want to know?"

"Well, seeing as how you want this to be short, I hope this question is a good one!" the reporter laughed. Then he went on. "You've now won five Olympic gold medals over the span of the last two Olympics. Americans realize this might be your last Olympic competition, and we're all very proud of you. What you have done is phenomenal."

"Thank you," said Kim.

"So here's my question," the reporter said. "Which gold is your favorite?"

Kim paused and felt the newest medal that lay around her neck. "This may surprise you, but none of the Olympic medals is my favorite. My favorite "gold" is a nugget most people would call 'Fool's Gold.'" She put her hand in her pocket and pulled it out for the reporter to see.

"I carry this wherever I go. It even goes up to the starting blocks with me. Do you want the story?" Kim smiled at the reporter.

The man leaned forward. "Tell me about it, would you?" And he turned on his tape recorder. This sounded like it could be even a bigger scoop than he'd hoped for.

"I grew up on a cattle farm in Colorado," Kim began, "where the aspen trees grew on the hillsides, and the snow peaks jutted up in the sky in any direction you looked. My brother is two years older than I am, and we used to ride horses after school every day. Like most older brothers, he was always acting superior and telling me how unskilled I was at everything. You know how sibling rivalry is."

The threesome laughed, and Kim continued. "One afternoon, we were riding far away from our usual spot, high up in the mountains. The area had once been a place where gold miners had found huge veins of gold. The gold mine itself had been closed long ago for safety reasons, but we knew it was right around where we were.

"We sat on our horses on top of a hill that overlooked the valley below and looked for herds of elk. We didn't find any, so we just enjoyed the view. My horse loved to munch on grass, but since we had a lot farther to go and I didn't want his stomach to get upset, I pulled on the reigns to point his head away from a clump of grass near a pile of rocks. That's when I saw this shiny nugget.

"Don't be **too** impressed. It's fool's gold."

What do you think her brother's reaction will be to her find? Read on.

"When I saw that rock gleaming brightly in the sunlight, I yelled out what every kid would: 'I found a gold nugget!'

"But my older brother laughed at me and said, 'More likely it's just fool's gold.'

"That started an argument that lasted through our lunch. While we ate our sandwiches and graham crackers, we were still yelling, in between bites.

'It *is* gold!' I said.

'It is *not!*' he yelled back.

'IT IS!'

'IS NOT!'

"The next day, I took the nugget to school with me. I was on the playground showing it to all my friends, and everyone was admiring it. Then my brother walked over with two of his friends and loudly announced, 'Don't be too impressed. It's fool's gold.'

"Then everyone laughed and walked away. Even my best girlfriends were embarrassed for me and walked away. I stood there alone, feeling really ashamed. That day I went home crying. I didn't even want to eat dinner, I was so embarrassed. Finally, my father came upstairs to my room to talk to me.

"He said, 'Kim, I know you're really proud of that nugget you found.'

"I shook my head, because now I only felt embarrassed. I had found fool's gold and thought it was something it wasn't. But I didn't say anything because I was afraid I would start crying. I didn't want my father to see me do that.

"He asked, 'Were you proud of the nugget when you found it?'

"I nodded. He said, 'So it was special to you, then?'

"I heard myself reply, 'Yes, it was so beautiful. I was very proud of finding it.'

"'Then,' he said, 'it doesn't matter if it's real or not, does it? If it's real to you, then it has its own special quality. It's what you believe that counts.'

"I swallowed my tears and nodded. I looked at the gold nugget. It looked real to me. And so what if it wasn't real? It was still beautiful. It didn't matter if it was worth two hundred dollars or two cents. It had meaning to me.

What do you think about her father's response to her gold nugget?

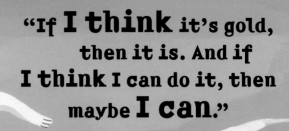

"If **I think** it's gold, then it is. And if I think I can do it, then maybe **I can.**"

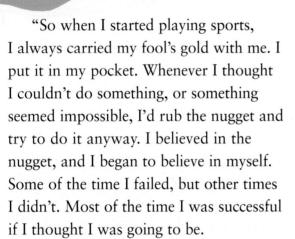

"So when I started playing sports, I always carried my fool's gold with me. I put it in my pocket. Whenever I thought I couldn't do something, or something seemed impossible, I'd rub the nugget and try to do it anyway. I believed in the nugget, and I began to believe in myself. Some of the time I failed, but other times I didn't. Most of the time I was successful if I thought I was going to be.

"When I was ten, I watched the Olympics on TV. After I saw the women in the running events, I told my brother that I was going to be a runner like that one day. He said it was impossible, that only superheroes or special people get to do extraordinary things like go to the Olympics.

"I had that gold nugget in my pocket. I rubbed it, and I said to myself, 'If I THINK it's gold, then it is. And if I think I can do it, then maybe I can.'

"When I was fifteen, I was a really fast runner, and everyone said I was full of promise. Then one day I fell off my horse and hurt my knee and shoulder. My doctor told me I had to stop running for a while, and I might not be able to compete anymore. But I don't think I really ever believed the doctor. I had my nugget, you see, and I still believed in myself.

"My doctor saw how determined I was, and so she prescribed physical therapy. She sent me to a swimming pool to improve my strength.

"I swam every day, although slowly at first. I swam and swam and kept swimming. Slowly, the muscles around my knee began to heal. My shoulder began to get stronger and stronger. Soon I was swimming in the morning and afternoon. And the strangest thing happened—I started to really enjoy swimming. The minute my body was submerged in water, I was happy.

"Two years later, I was in my first Olympic swimming trial."

How did Kim's physical therapy help her to become an Olympic swimmer?

"So *that's* why the nugget is your favorite! Is it really fool's gold, or is it real?" the reporter asked.

"You know, I never had anyone examine it. It may be real gold, and it may not be. I don't know, and to tell you the truth, I don't want to know! I know what I believe it to be."

Then the reporter said, "Can I ask just one more question to follow up what you've already said?"

"Go ahead."

"Are you still angry at your brother for embarrassing you in front of your friends?"

"Absolutely not," the swimmer said. "I thank my older brother, because if I hadn't learned that lesson, I might not have become the person I am. I certainly wouldn't be speaking with a reporter!"

**"It helped me believe in myself."**

"Fool's gold . . . " the reporter mused. "Could you be saying that you actually fooled yourself into thinking you could win the race?"

"No, not at all! I'm saying that this gold nugget helped me do something more important. It helped me *believe* in myself."

The swimming coach leaned over and hugged Kim. He said to her, "I'm so proud of you. Why didn't you ever tell me this story before?"

Kim put her hand over her coach's. "Well, big brother, I was waiting for the perfect time!" ○

# Stop and Respond

## Who's the Fool Now?

Carmaker Henry Ford, basketball star Michael Jordan, artist Vincent van Gogh, and pop superstar Madonna have something in common. When they first started their careers, people said they were following foolish dreams. Research a famous person. What were their dreams when they were growing up? Were they foolish dreams or not?

## Foolish or Brave?

In a group, debate one of the following actions as either foolish or brave: mountain climbing, skydiving, downhill skiing, becoming a stunt person, or becoming a firefighter. State at least three reasons why you feel the way you do.

## When Life Gives You Lemons . . .

If you are like everyone else, you have suffered through at least a few embarrassing moments. Think of one that eventually taught you an important lesson. Write about it in your journal, and share the lesson you learned with a friend.

# The Mystery of the
# Mima Mounds

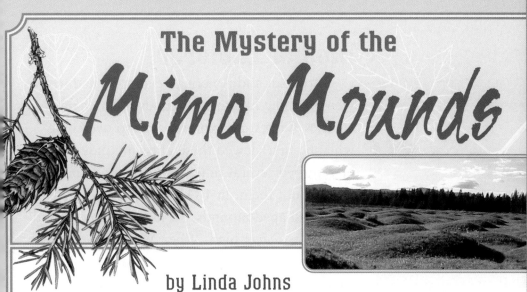

## by Linda Johns

Henry trudged along. His mom had promised that this would be "a hike with a bit of mystery mixed in." The only mystery so far was how much longer they'd walk before they stopped for sandwiches.

"This is like every other hike we've gone on this summer," Henry called ahead to his mom.

"Once we get to the bottom of this hill, things will open up. You'll see it for yourself," his mom said.

See what? Henry couldn't imagine anything opening up. There were miles and miles of forest everywhere he looked.

Five minutes later, the Douglas fir trees thinned out. They were now out of the woods and looking out at an unexpected sight—a huge prairie. This half of Washington state was heavy with forests, so one didn't expect to see prairies.

A closer look revealed something even stranger.

"What in the world are those?" Laura asked.

His sister had taken her headphones off. Henry had almost forgotten she was with them.

"It looks like it was invaded by gophers from outer space," Laura said.

The children were mesmerized. They were staring at hundreds and hundreds of prairie bumps. The entire grassy area was covered with gently rolling hills. But "hill" was too big of a word for them, Henry thought. They were really more like big bumps or mounds.

"They look like gigantic gopher mounds," Henry said.

Each "hill" was about 6 feet high.

"Must have been some huge gophers," Laura said.

"Maybe they're monster mole hills. Or maybe some gigantic mutant rodents made them and they still live inside!" Henry said.

"Ewww!" said Laura.

"These are called Mima mounds, named after a Native American word," said their mother. "Can you think of any other reasons the ground might be shaped like this?"

Henry's mother was a scientist. She was always trying to get them to think of possibilities and then try to prove them. He didn't mind this time.

"Something to do with Native American ceremonies?" asked Henry.

"A weird kind of farming?" asked Laura.

"Alien invasion? Ice age formation? Earthquake?" Henry rattled off his thoughts.

"For the past 200 years, scientists have been coming up with all kinds of theories about the Mima mounds, including the ones you've just suggested," said Henry's mom . . .

Mima Mounds

Above: Each mound in the Mima Mound Natural Preserve reaches 4 to 6 feet tall. No one knows for sure how or when these mounds appeared.
Right: Camas flower

## Mima Mounds

Mima mounds are found in the states of Washington and Minnesota and in other parts of the world. They are definitely an oddity.

How do you think the Mima mounds were formed? Read on for more information.

They appear in flat, grassy areas. There isn't just one Mima mound, though. There are hundreds and hundreds—sometimes even thousands. In fact, in one part of Washington, there used to be millions of these mounds. They looked like a layer of huge goose bumps stretched across the land.

## Mound Explorers

European and American explorers had never seen anything like these mounds. Lieutenant Charles Wilkes, an explorer, was so overcome when he first viewed these grass mounds that he returned several times to dig around and write about them. In 1841, he described them as cone-shaped mounds, 30 feet in diameter and about 6 to 7 feet high. When Wilkes opened up three of the mounds, he discovered nothing but round stones in them.

Wilkes' first theory had been that the mounds were some sort of Native American burial ground. But no relics or artifacts were found inside the mounds. Still, he refused to believe that the mounds were natural. He then thought that the mounds were tied to Native American traditions, since a local tribe was farming in the area. Later, Wilkes concluded that earlier tribes must have created the mounds.

Others have thought the Mima mounds were made by people, too. One theory is that Native American tribes created the mounds to use for farming camas bulbs. Camas was an important plant that was used as both food and medicine. They had large, beautiful blooms, and so each year, the little hills of the Mima mounds bloomed with color. Today, scientists believe that Native American tribes made use of the Mima mounds, but they did not create them.

So the question remains: Who or what *did* make these mysterious mounds?

## An Animal Hotel?

Over the years, many people have been convinced that animals burrowed inside these mounds. Some scientists also believed that animals made them, too. But what kind of animal could make a series of 6-foot tall mounds? It would take a gaggle of gigantic gophers, an abundant army of ants, or some unidentified monster rodent to do that kind of work. Remember, this isn't just one little mound. There used to be thousands—even millions—of them.

Rodents, gophers, ants, ground squirrels, and giant toads have all been named as the culprits, at one time or another, by scientists looking for answers to the mystery of the Mima mounds.

Giant toads actually do play a role in some Mima mounds found in the state of Minnesota. The toads didn't make the mounds, but they are certainly making good use of them.

OK, the toads aren't really gigantic. But they are large for toads. These Canadian toads grow to be about 3 inches tall. At the end of the summer, they migrate south to Minnesota and make their homes in the Mima mounds in Schaefer Prairie. The Minnesota winters may be cold, but the Mima mounds make warm homes for toads. Each mound can be home to hundreds of toads. The toads dig through the sides and then dig down underneath the mounds. The mounds give them extra insulation to keep warm. Hundreds of toad bodies all curled up together gives them extra warmth, too.

The Mima mounds of Minnesota are a bit smaller than the ones in Washington. But both mounds have attracted some strange theories over the years. One early theory was that a kind of sucker fish made these hills. That theory really had no proof to back it up and now seems a bit silly.

What do *you* think about the animal theories? Why do you think that?

## Icy Thoughts

Ice age theories often crop up when talking about the Mima mounds. The most popular theory over recent years involves a big freeze that occurred fourteen thousand years ago. Many geologists think that a glacier covered an area of Washington during the last ice age. When the subzero temperatures rose, the glacier began to melt and leave behind gravel and silt, which froze and then thawed. This ongoing cycle would have made the earth crack and bulge, perhaps causing the mounds to form.

But how can this theory explain the similar size and placement of the mounds? Perhaps that's one reason why scientists still can't agree on exactly what made the Mima mounds. Most scientists, however, do agree that the Mima mounds are a geological formation, and not the work of burrowing gophers, sucker fish, or even giant toads.

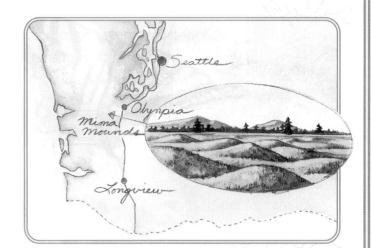

Above: Mima mounds nature area

# PLAYING IT COOL IN THE FACE OF DANGER

**Can you see the katydid?**

When it comes to animals, it's a dog-eat-dog world. Or make that a snake-eat-mouse world. Or a tiger-eat-zebra world . . . you get the picture. With all of this hunting and stalking going on in the wild, it's no wonder that some animals have adapted clever ways to fool predators.

Just try to see a green grasshopper on a leaf, a brown chameleon on a tree branch, or a gray toad in damp leaves. The coloring of these animals makes them hard to see in their habitats. Some insects are experts at hiding. Their bodies are shaped like leaves, twigs, or even bird droppings! Blending into the background is called *camouflage*. Camouflage keeps animals safe from predators.

Other animals don't bother with hiding—they could be award-winning actors instead. Take the Australian frilled lizard, for example. When it's calm, cool, and collected, it looks like an ordinary lizard. But if another animal messes with it, the lizard spreads out a big flap of skin around its neck and opens its mouth wide. Yikes!

Still others simply play dead. Opossums are famous for "playing dead" when they're threatened. Ever hear the expression "playing possum?" Like the opossum, the Eastern hognose snake lies on its back, looking lifeless, when danger looms. Predators think, "What's the use?" and move along. And the clever animal avoids being someone's lunch for another day.

So the next time you are hiking, be on the lookout. You may be fooled by nature. Perhaps there are more creatures to see than first meets the eye.

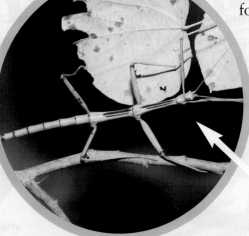

**Can you see the walkingstick?**

COMPREHENSION QUARTERLY 5

# CQ

ISSUE D: Monitoring

# The Main Character

# The Main Character

## THINK ABOUT: Monitoring

**D4**

FICTION
### Remembering Guthrie
What do a girl and a gorilla have in common? Read about this unusual friendship.

**D11**

NONFICTION
### The Gift of Life
Find out how Brandon gets the chance to lead a normal life.

NONFICTION
### The Forgotten Man of Gettysburg
Learn about the person whom history has failed to remember.

**D19**

**D25**

FICTION
### Helping Hands
Follow Sammy in his quest to do good.

MONITORING

# What a Great Character!

Sonia was spending Saturday morning at the library. She flipped through the pages of a novel, trying to decide if she wanted to read it. *I'll bet I won't like Daisy,* she thought to herself. *She's got a swimming pool, closets full of clothes, and her own Arabian horse.* Even though Sonia didn't think she and Daisy had anything in common, something about the book looked interesting, so she checked it out.

Later that day, Sonia sat down to read. Since this was a novel for teenagers and she was only ten, she knew it would be especially important for her to **monitor** her reading, or check to make sure she understood everything. As she read, she wondered about Daisy. She asked herself lots of questions about the character, including these: Can Daisy really be as stuck-up as she seems? Why doesn't she want to go to the party? Questions bubbled up in Sonia's mind. They came from her own experience and from ideas the author included in her writing.

As Sonia continued reading, she made some discoveries about Daisy. She learned that Daisy wasn't stuck-up at all—just shy. She found out that Daisy's family moved frequently because of her parents' jobs. Sonia started changing her mind about Daisy as she read on. Sonia began liking Daisy more and more and wondering what was going to happen to her.

By the time she was finished reading the novel, Sonia was rooting for Daisy, who had turned out to be an interesting and complicated character with plenty of good qualities. That night, Sonia wrote in her journal: "I'm sure glad I read this book. It's a cool book, and Daisy is a great character. I really changed my mind about her!"

Think about a time you changed your mind as you read. Perhaps you read facts you hadn't known before, or perhaps you read an opinion that persuaded you to change your mind. So when you read, keep an open mind. You may need to change your thinking!

# Remembering Guthrie

by Tamim Ansary

**E**rin Carter clutched her mother's hand as they strolled across the lawn. It was a crisp day but warm enough that people were walking around in T-shirts. Winter was never like this in New England. Erin was glad she and her mother had come to California to see Uncle Peter, here at the university where he taught.

"How's Billy?" Uncle Peter asked.

Billy was Erin's little brother. One year ago, when Billy was only three, doctors had discovered he was deaf. "He's quite well, really," Erin's mother, Maggie, said. "We're all learning sign language now, so we'll be able to communicate as a family. Billy, of course, signs quite well, and Erin is learning quickly. It's James and I who are having difficulties, I'm afraid."

"Well," said Uncle Peter, "it's always harder for adults to learn a language."

Just then a car pulled up in front of the science building, and a woman got out. She turned to help someone else—it was a powerful ape with black fur. Pedestrians stopped to gawk. Erin gasped.

"No need to be frightened!" Uncle Peter laughed. "That's Ginger."

But Erin was shivering with fear. When the ape turned toward her, she could not hold back a scream. Maggie quickly dragged her eleven-year-old daughter onto a new path, away from the frightening sight. "Let's see what's over here," she chirped in a bright, false voice.

Later, in the privacy of Uncle Peter's kitchen, the adults discussed the event. Erin was lying down in the next room, and they thought she was asleep; but she was only half asleep, and the half that wasn't asleep could hear them talking.

"Erin is going through a phase," her mom was telling her uncle. "Ever since Guthrie . . . "

"Who's Guthrie?" Uncle Peter asked.

"Didn't I tell you? He was a pet—an old tomcat we used to have. A year ago, a car struck him outside our house. Erin and one of her classmates saw it happen. They tried to get the poor creature to the vet, but . . . it was too late. Erin has been having nightmares ever since. She needs to get past it somehow—that's one reason why I brought her with me, Peter. I thought the trip might help her forget."

Forget, thought Erin, feeling numb. They kept telling her to forget. She loved Guthrie. How could she forget him? Didn't they see how important it was to remember? Why couldn't anyone understand?

In the next room, her mother sighed. "Ever since Guthrie died, she's been troubled by a lot of childhood fears. You know—she can't sleep in the dark. She's afraid of snakes, spiders, gorillas—"

"Gorillas!" Peter exclaimed. "Why gorillas?"

"Because they're terrifying creatures, aren't they? Why, I just read a survey that asked children what creature they feared the most, and gorillas came in third—just behind snakes and spiders."

> What do you know about gorillas?

"That's ridiculous," Peter fumed. "Gorillas don't hurt anybody."

"Ah, but they could," said his sister, "couldn't they? They're strong enough. I don't mind telling you, Peter. I felt a shiver myself, seeing that brute running around loose. Surely the government could see to it that—"

"Ginger was *not* running around loose! Dr. Loden was right there—"

"That slip of a girl?" Maggie scoffed. "What could she do if that monkey went on a rampage? I mean no criticism, Peter, but—"

"Gorillas are apes, Maggie, not monkeys. Just because they're both bipeds doesn't mean they're the same. And you've got quite the wrong idea about Ginger. Angela Loden—well, she's teaching Ginger to talk."

"Teaching a gorilla to talk?" Maggie burst into laughter. "Now I know you're pulling my leg. Do gorillas even have voices? Except to roar, I mean?"

"That's just the point. They may not have the vocal chords needed for speech, but that's why Dr. Loden is teaching Ginger to use sign language."

"Sign language! You mean, like we use with Billy?"

"Exactly. That's one way a creature without a voice might communicate—if it has the brains. The experiment has been very successful. Ginger knows about 500 signs now. Of course, some signs had to be adapted for Ginger because gorillas have smaller thumbs than people do, you know, so they can't make the same signs we do, or at least not the same way. But Ginger can carry on a conversation. Say, why don't we go over there tomorrow? It would do Erin good to see that Ginger is not the brute she imagines."

"Oh, Peter! I don't know . . . ," Maggie began, but Erin herself was in the doorway now.

"I want to, Mom. Can we?" she pleaded.

Angela Loden had a comfortable house near the university. She was in the kitchen when they arrived. "You're just in time," she said. "I'm preparing Ginger's lunch. Give me a minute and then we'll go in and see her."

Dr. Loden finished arranging raw vegetables on a platter and led the way into a comfortable room with a low ceiling. Ginger was on the floor surrounded by a heap of toys. She was manipulating some kind of gadget and stopped when the visitors entered.

"Ginger," said Dr. Loden, "these people would like to meet you."

The gorilla made a gesture with both thumbs.

"Hey—she says we stink!" Erin burst out indignantly.

Angela Loden looked embarrassed. "Oh, Ginger! Be nice. Look, I've made some lunch." And to Erin, she said, "You must excuse Ginger. She's been going through a difficult time recently."

Ginger trudged to the table, climbed onto a chair, and then turned to Dr. Loden and made a series of signs.

"She says she's hungry and the food looks good," Dr. Loden translated.

"I know," said Erin. Dr. Loden's diplomacy had worked. Ginger seemed relaxed. Erin had stopped trembling, and her detachment was giving way to curiosity. Up close, Ginger did not seem so big or wild after all—not like those awful beasts in . . . what was that movie called? *Jungle Beast*.

"You see, Erin," Dr. Loden said softly, "Ginger lost someone that was dear to her. She had a kitten—"

"Perhaps we should change the subject," Maggie cut in.

> How have you changed your mind about gorillas?

"What kitten? What happened to it?" Erin asked.

Dr. Loden cleared her throat. "Well, perhaps we should talk about something else."

But Erin moved to the table and sat down across from Ginger. She didn't need anyone to translate for her. She knew how to sign. She could talk to the gorilla herself. In sign language, she asked, "What happened to your cat?"

"Gone," Ginger signed. "Sleeping now. Sleeping."

At that, Erin felt tears coming up, rising out of the sadness that never seemed to go away.

But then, she didn't want it to go away because she didn't want to forget poor Guthrie. What was the use of being loved if people could forget you?

"What was your cat's name?" she signed.

Ginger sucked in her large lower lip and looked around. She picked up a yellow rubber duck and squeezed it. Then she signed, "Squeak. Good cat. Squeak gone now. Ginger sad."

Does this make sense to you that a gorilla can use sign language? Why or why not?

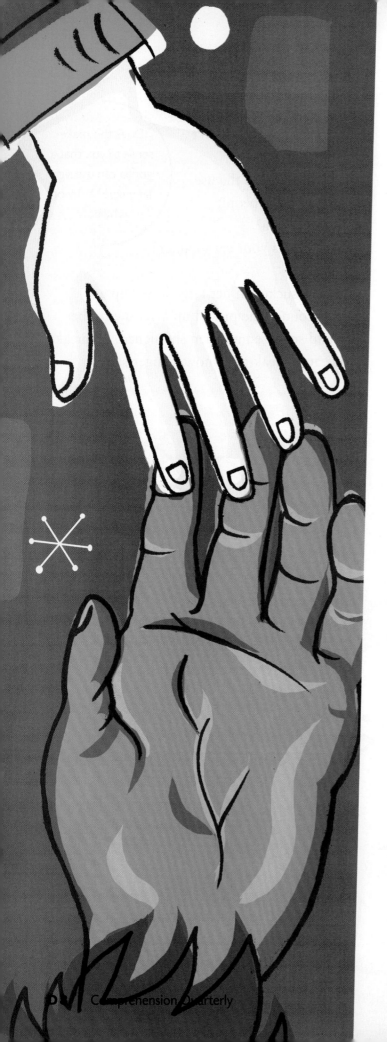

Erin nodded. She knew all about that sadness. Every day when she came home from school, she expected to see Guthrie on the window sill, but he was never there. It wasn't like her mind really thought he would be. Guthrie would never come back—she knew that. She just didn't think that was a good reason to forget him. How could they even ask her to do that? What if she herself had to go away? She didn't want to be forgotten!

"What happened to Squeak?" she signed.

"Gone," the gorilla signed again. "Ginger cry."

"Me too," said Erin. As she spoke the words, she felt as if her heart would break. "Will you forget her, Ginger?" And she signed, "Forget?"

Behind Erin, no one spoke.

"Forget?" Erin signed. "Forget Squeak?"

Ginger shook her head vigorously and a deep warmth suddenly filled Erin. At last! Someone understood! "Me neither," she signed. Out loud she said, "I had a cat named Guthrie, and he's gone now, but I'm always going to remember him."

> What did you do when you came to the word *vigorously*? How did you know what it means?

Ginger reached across the table and set her large leathery hand on Erin's much smaller one. "Good talk," she signed with her other hand. "Good you. Ginger love."

Laughing through her tears, Erin said, "Oh, Ginger, I'm never going to forget you, either." ●

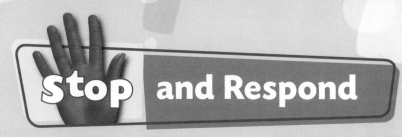

# Stop and Respond

## Think Again

As you read "Remembering Guthrie," what did you learn about Ginger that surprised you? How did some of your ideas about gorillas change as you read the story? Make a two-column chart. In the first column under the heading "Ideas I Had," write some ideas you used to have about gorillas. In the second column under the heading "Ideas I Have Now," list how your ideas changed as you read about Ginger.

## Testing 1,2,3

Make up a multiple choice test to find out how well readers understood "Remembering Guthrie." Write at least five questions and provide four possible answers (one of them correct) for each question. Then have a classmate take the test. Do you both agree which answers were correct?

## A Picture is Worth a Thousand Words

When Erin returns home, she will probably want to tell Billy all about Ginger. Think of three words that Erin might use to describe Ginger. Fold a piece of paper in thirds and write each descriptive word in a column. Draw a picture to go with each word. You may want to find out how to communicate these words using American Sign Language.

# The Name Game

We all have a first name and a last name. Many of us also have a middle name. Our name identifies us as a unique person. It sets us apart from other people.

Many parents take a lot of time in picking just the right name for their child. They read baby name books, search online sources, and ask for suggestions from family and friends.

Many people believe that your name is a reflection of your character. They also believe that names have power. Whatever your name is, be proud of it. It is your source of identity. It is you!

**Ten Most Popular Names from 1900–1909**

| | Male | Female |
|---|---|---|
| 1. | John | Mary |
| 2. | William | Helen |
| 3. | James | Margaret |
| 4. | George | Anna |
| 5. | Joseph | Ruth |
| 6. | Charles | Elizabeth |
| 7. | Robert | Dorothy |
| 8. | Frank | Marie |
| 9. | Edward | Mildred |
| 10. | Henry | Alice |

**Ten Most Popular Names in 2000**

| | Male | Female |
|---|---|---|
| 1. | Michael | Hannah |
| 2. | Jacob | Emily |
| 3. | Matthew | Madison |
| 4. | Joseph | Elizabeth |
| 5. | Christopher | Alexis |
| 6. | Nicholas | Sarah |
| 7. | Andrew | Taylor |
| 8. | William | Lauren |
| 9. | Joshua | Jessica |
| 10. | Daniel | Ashley |

# The Gift of Life

*by Denise M. Jordan*

Brandon pounded out the rhythm and the crowd started rocking. He swayed in time to the beat as his drumsticks flew. His buddies in the pep band, Too Good, backed him up. It was halftime. The gym was filled with the sounds of high school basketball and the rhythm of James Brown's "I Feel Good."

"I Feel Good" could almost be Brandon's theme song. The sixteen-year-old high school sophomore is feeling pretty good these days. But it hasn't always been that way.

When Brandon was three weeks old, his parents took him to the emergency room at the local hospital. They weren't sure what was wrong with him, but they knew something wasn't right. X rays and ultrasounds, special techniques that allow doctors to picture the inside of the body, showed that Brandon's kidneys and bladder were not filtering and draining waste products as they should.

The pediatrician declared that Brandon needed surgery immediately— surgery that could not be obtained in their

What do you know about the kidneys? What do you think the author will tell you about Brandon's kidneys?

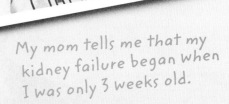

*My mom tells me that my kidney failure began when I was only 3 weeks old.*

My parents and my brother, Lawrence, have been very helpful and supportive throughout my recovery.

hometown, Lansing, Michigan. The doctor wanted Brandon airlifted to Children's Hospital in Detroit and ordered a helicopter. Brandon's concerned parents turned down the chopper; they didn't want to wait. They jumped in their car and rushed their sick baby to Detroit themselves. They were escorted by an ambulance with its sirens wailing all the way.

Brandon's parents were told that his kidneys would never work properly. At the hospital, he received the first of many laboratory tests, X rays, medical procedures, and surgeries.

Because of Brandon's poor kidney development, unwanted substances that the kidneys normally filter out and get rid of, remained in his body. The poor filtering also led to problems with a blood disorder called anemia. The anemia caused Brandon to tire easily. He was not allowed to play any contact sports. No wrestling. No football. No roughhousing. He could not risk more damage to his kidneys.

Brandon decided he was not going to live life on the sidelines. "I decided not to focus on what I couldn't do. I thought it better to focus on what I could do."

He shot hoops in the driveway with his older brother and friends. He learned to play soccer. He learned to play the drums. And when his parents weren't looking, he got into pickup games of touch football. When Brandon got tired, he rested.

Is this what you thought the author would tell you about Brandon's life? Why or why not?

As Brandon grew older, his kidneys got worse. By the time he was thirteen, his kidneys were only working at about ten percent of where they should be if they were normal. His health was getting worse and the future looked grim. Brandon needed a new kidney. His name was placed on the transplant list. In the meantime, he went on dialysis.

Dialysis is a manmade way to filter body fluids. During dialysis, a solution is put into the abdomen through a small tube. The solution washes through the abdominal cavity, pulling waste products from the body. When the tube is opened, the solution and the waste products drain out. Dialysis does what the kidney cannot do. It's not 100 percent effective, but it is better than a defective kidney. Dialysis helps a kidney patient feel better and live longer.

Brandon's mother was taught to do the dialysis procedure at home. Every night, when Brandon went to bed, she set up the equipment and manipulated the tubes, bags, and other gadgets associated with home dialysis. Brandon had to lay still for several hours. He was ready to be still at night, but during the day he had too many things to do. He didn't want to miss school. He wanted to see his friends. He wanted to play his drums.

Brandon was on dialysis for three months. During this time, he followed a low salt and low protein diet. Salt was limited because salt caused his body to swell with water— water that his defective kidneys could not manage. Proteins, such as dairy products, peanut butter, and salted nuts, were limited because the waste products can cause more kidney damage and harm other body organs.

Meanwhile, Brandon's father was preparing to donate one of his healthy kidneys to Brandon. "We knew that at some point in time, it would come down to a kidney transplant," explained Brandon's father. "I made the decision that when the time came, I would donate a kidney."

Brandon's father had to be tested to make sure that his kidney was a good match for Brandon. If it was not, Brandon would not be able to use his father's kidney. Doctors looked at the internal makeup of Brandon and his father. They checked the blood type and the DNA structure of their cells to see if the two of them were similar. Blood and tissue samples were taken from each of them.

After several months of testing, the doctors determined that Brandon's father was a good match. Brandon and his family made the trip to Children's Hospital in Detroit, Michigan, for the transplant procedure.

"I was scared at first," admitted Brandon. He didn't know what to expect, and he had already been through a number of painful procedures in his thirteen years. "It didn't

> What do you know about donating kidneys? What do you think the author will tell you about this?

In my sophomore year of high school, I decided to join the marching and pep bands. I learned how to play the drums and the cymbals.

This is a photo of my brother and me after the Spring 2001 Orchestra Concert.

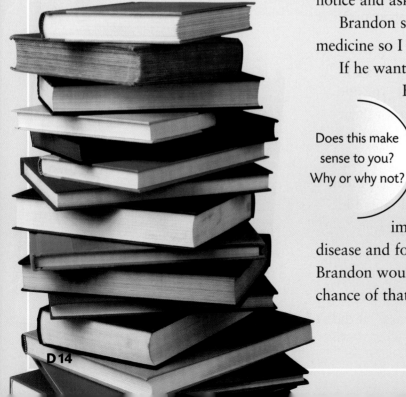

hurt as much as I thought it would," said Brandon. "After it was all over, I had this big scar, but it wasn't that bad."

Brandon doesn't remember much about the transplant procedure, but he does remember the trip to the operating room. "As we were going down to the operating room, my dad was cracking jokes," reported Brandon. "He had everybody laughing, but that's how my dad is. He's always telling jokes."

Brandon spent about ten days in the hospital. "Most people stay three weeks," said Brandon, "but I healed so fast, they let me go home early." Brandon says he feels a hundred times better now than he did before the transplant. He has more energy. "I go a lot more places now. I go to parties. I play in the marching band at my high school, and I play in the pep band, Too Good."

Brandon's also doing better in school. He's able to concentrate better. When he was so ill with his kidney disease and his body chemistry was out of balance, he had difficulty concentrating on school work. Now that he's feeling better, he can give school his full attention.

Brandon still has to be careful with his health. He tries to follow a healthy diet and take his medication as directed. Taking the medication is the hard part. Brandon has to take about eight different pills every day at scheduled times. He even has to take the medicine at school. His classmates notice and ask, "Why are you always taking medicine?"

Brandon shrugs it off and simply explains, "I take the medicine so I can feel good."

If he wanted to give a more thorough explanation, Brandon could tell them about the threat of a transplant rejection. Even though his father's kidney was a great match, it's possible that Brandon's body might reject the new kidney. Rejection occurs when the body considers a new organ to be a foreign invader. Brandon's immune system, the body's defense against disease and foreign objects, would attack the new organ and Brandon would get very sick. The medication reduces the chance of that happening.

Does this make sense to you? Why or why not?

"It's a lot, but you've got to do it," said Brandon. "I'm used to it now." Brandon was lucky that his father was willing and able to donate a kidney. Family members often make the best matches, but they aren't always healthy enough to donate. People can wait years before an organ becomes available. It's a particular problem for African Americans because there's a shortage of African American donors.

In most organ transplants, size is the important factor. When it comes to kidneys, genes are more important. Kidneys from people with the same ethnic background match better and there is less chance of rejection.

How have you changed your mind about organ transplants?

"The kidney transplant gave me a second chance on life," declared Brandon. He intends to take full advantage of it. He still can't wrestle or play football. He can't play on the soccer team. But he is thinking about trying out for his high school's baseball team. ○

There are two kinds of organ donors—living and cadaverous. A living donor is someone like Brandon's father. He acknowledged the need for the organ and donated it. A cadaverous donor is someone like a seventeen-year-old girl from South Bend, Indiana, who died as a result of an auto accident.

The girl's mother received a phone call late one night. She was told that her daughter had been seriously injured in a car accident. When the mother arrived at the hospital, she was given worse news. Hospital respirators, machines to aid breathing, and other emergency equipment were temporarily keeping her seventeen-year-old daughter's body going. The girl's mother was asked if she wanted to donate her daughter's organs.

"We had discussed organ donation in our family," said the girl's mother, "and my daughter had signed on her driver's license as an organ donor." The mother agreed to the donation. She doesn't know the names of the people that received her daughter's organs. She just knows they helped someone.

I am very thankful that my father was able to donate his kidney to me. If it wasn't for him, I would not have my health today.

# Stop and Respond

## What I Thought I Knew

List at least four ideas you had about organ transplants and organ donors before you read the story. Put a check mark by the ideas that were confirmed in the story. Cross out any of your ideas that turned out to be inaccurate. Then write a letter to Brandon telling how you changed your mind about organ transplants and organ donors.

## Character Traits Web

Make a Character Traits Web to describe Brandon. Write *Brandon* at the center of the web. Then write four character traits that describe him. In the box under each trait, write examples from the story that show the trait.

Trait: brave
Example:

Trait:
Example:

Brandon

Trait:
Example:

Trait:
Example:

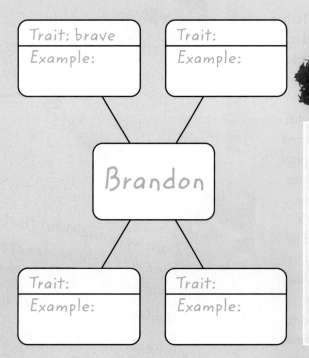

## Make a Difference

Organ donations are one way to make a difference in someone's life. In a small group, brainstorm ways you could make a difference in your school or community. List things you could do individually or as a group. Then make a poster to illustrate one of your ideas.

# Kokomo Jr.

## What a Character!

Some main characters can definitely be called "characters." In the early days of television, when programs were viewed "live," a chimpanzee by the name of Kokomo Jr. appeared on an early morning news show. He became very popular with viewers and quickly gained fame all across the country.

Kokomo Jr. has met presidents and first ladies, politicians, and actors. He has made personal appearances for many charities and has visited elementary schools. He has appeared in over 12 movies and over 20 television shows. He has also made numerous television commercials. He was the first chimp to have his picture on a greeting card.

Kokomo Jr. is retired from show business now and lives in comfort in North Carolina. He likes to spend his days playing outside and riding his tricycle. He is also interested in painting. You can buy his art on the Internet!

## MONITORING

# Let's Find Out

When Tomas learned that his little brother, Silvio, might need a kidney transplant, he was upset. Tomas decided to find out what he could about kidney transplants. To him, learning about kidney transplants was the best way not to be scared of them.

The first place Tomas turned for information was the encyclopedia. The topic of kidney transplants is complicated, and his family's encyclopedia was written for adults. But Tomas was pretty sure he could understand the entry on kidney transplants if he **monitored** his reading and used all the fix-up strategies he knew for any parts of the article he was having trouble understanding.

Tomas read the article straight through to get the main idea. He adjusted his reading rate—reading the article more slowly than he would read a novel. He knew reading slowly and carefully would help him understand the difficult ideas and hard words.

After Tomas finished reading the entry, he reread some parts that had puzzled him. Here is one sentence he reread and what Tomas said to himself as he read it.

> When someone's kidneys deteriorate, in spite of receiving conventional treatments, the person becomes weak and anemic.

I don't know exactly what *deteriorate* means, but it must mean "get worse," since the sentence says the person becomes weak. *Conventional* usually means "ordinary." Maybe it means "standard" here. I know what being anemic is. That's when a person doesn't get enough iron, so they get pale and tired.

Tomas learned a lot about kidney transplants by reading the encyclopedia entry. He found out that people have been getting successful kidney transplants for more than 40 years. When Tomas was through reading, he reviewed what he had read and jotted down a few questions to ask his parents.

Think about a time when you read something difficult but important. What fix-up strategies did you use to understand and monitor what you read?

# The Forgotten Man of Gettysburg

### BY DAVID R. COLLINS

"Four score and seven years ago our fathers brought forth . . . "

These words began one of the most memorable speeches ever delivered—and one of the shortest as well. Most Americans could quickly identify it as the The Gettysburg Address and its author as Abraham Lincoln. The occasion for its delivery was the formal dedication of a National Soldiers' Cemetery on November 19, 1863.

But as time has put Lincoln and his Gettysburg Address into the lasting historical spotlight, the other individuals and events of that dedication day have been forgotten.

Strangely enough, Abraham Lincoln was not the principal speaker at the dedication ceremonies. No, the main speaker and attraction was one of the most beloved Americans of his time, Edward Everett.

**Inset:** Portrait of Edward Everett

**Background:** Battlefield at Gettysburg, Pennsylvania

Born while George Washington was president, Edward Everett was sixty-nine years old when he was selected by Pennsylvania officials to be the principal orator at Gettysburg. Edward Everett was well qualified for the task. Often called the "pride of Massachusetts," he had served as governor of the state and had represented Massachusetts in both the United States House of Representatives and Senate. He had also been ambassador to England and president of Harvard University.

But it was in the world of words that Edward Everett had earned the great respect of his countrymen. An admirer of George Washington, Everett gave frequent lectures on the first president. Publishers were eager to purchase Everett's speeches, and four volumes of them had been put together. Money from the sale of these books helped to purchase Mount Vernon, George Washington's home, as a permanent national memorial.

Edward Everett had two full months to prepare himself for the ceremonies at Gettysburg. He did not waste a moment. He carefully studied the site where he was to speak—a flat meadow surrounded by peach orchards, wheat fields, and gentle hills rising upward to become the Allegheny Mountains.

While writing his speech, Everett often wondered if President Lincoln would be invited to Gettysburg. Under usual circumstances, the president would be an automatic guest for such a prestigious ceremony. But these were no usual circumstances. For more than two years the country had been at war.

Does how Everett prepares for his speech make sense to you? Why or why not?

**Below:** In 1860, Edward Everett was the Constitutional Union Party's candidate for Vice President. This song was written for his campaign.

**Background:** More than 15,000 people gathered at Gettysburg for the dedication ceremonies.

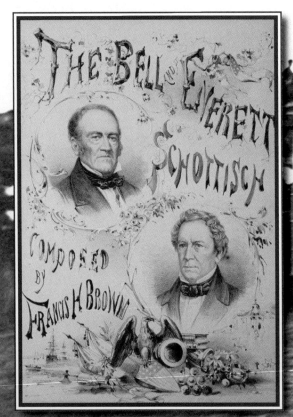

The Civil War had soured the mood of many Americans. Too often they had buried their friends and family. President Lincoln had become a symbol of sadness. Most of the Pennsylvania officials thought it would be better if Lincoln did not speak at the cemetery's dedication. Still, not to invite the President would be an inexcusable breach of diplomatic etiquette. Finally, only two weeks before the ceremonies, a printed notice of the event was delivered to President Lincoln. By waiting so long, many hoped he would not be able to attend.

> What did you do when you came to *inexcusable breach of diplomatic etiquette?* How did you know what it means?

It was no secret that Edward Everett hoped Lincoln would be there. Everett was a great believer in the observance of proper diplomatic etiquette. In addition, he had considerable respect for the much criticized president.

A light breeze blew across the cemetery site as more than 15,000 people who had made the pilgrimage to Gettysburg gathered at the dedication ceremonies. As Everett began speaking, there was silence in the crowd.

"Overlooking these broad fields now reposing from the labors of the waning year, the mighty Alleghenies dimly towering before us, the graves of our brethren beneath our feet, it is with hesitation that I raise my poor voice to break the eloquent silence of God and Nature . . . "

With a strong and forceful delivery, Everett continued speaking. He outlined the history of the war, defended the cause of one strong union over the cause of each state being sovereign, and reminded those present of the sacrifices each dead American soldier had made. For one hour and fifty-seven minutes, he spoke. When he had finished, the crowd applauded for many minutes. Then as Everett sat down, many people left. They had heard what they had come to hear.

Lincoln traveled by train from Washingtom, D.C. to Gettysburg. Some people believe that Lincoln is in this photo taken at Gettysburg.

President Lincoln, who had decided to attend the event, was the next person to speak. Many people in the crowd believed the president's words would not match the brilliance of Everett's speech.

"Four score and seven years ago . . . "

People in the meadow moved around, few of them listening to their president. Even several officials on the platform talked among themselves. But Edward Everett did not talk. He listened. He gave his wholehearted attention to each word that Lincoln spoke.

The Gettysburg Address lasted just under five minutes. The entire speech was ten sentences long. Across the country President Lincoln was criticized for his brief speech.

"Dull and ridiculous!" said some newspaper editors.

"Common and senseless!" echoed others.

Lincoln, himself, was disappointed with his address. Sadly he returned to Washington, feeling his speech was a failure. He felt that he had not succeeded at a time when he had deeply wanted to provide the people with a true picture of his heartfelt feelings.

But Edward Everett knew that President Lincoln had not failed. The next day he wrote this to his leader: "I should be glad if I could flatter myself that I came as near to the central idea of the occasion in two hours as you did in two minutes."

The kind words quickly cheered the disappointed Lincoln. When Everett, Lincoln's benefactor of kindness, made his praise of the president public, many people took a new look at Lincoln's Gettysburg Address. How meaningful the thoughts seemed.

Two years after the Gettysburg ceremonies, John Wilkes Booth, an actor, assassinated President Lincoln. His death brought reactions of grief from people all over the world.

Did you have to slow down or reread any parts of this article? Why or why not?

And in the same year, death took a man who lived in a wonderful world of words—Edward Everett, "the forgotten man of Gettysburg." ⬤

# The Battle of Gettysburg

The most important battle of the Civil War started because of shoes. Confederate generals heard that there was a supply of shoes in the prosperous enemy town of Gettysburg, Pennsylvania. Because many of the Confederate soldiers were marching barefoot, Gettysburg looked like a good place to get some shoes. Instead the Confederates ran into the Union Army and a battle began.

The Battle of Gettysburg lasted for three days (July 1–3, 1863). In those three days, over 23,000 Union soldiers were killed or wounded. More than 28,000 Confederates were killed, wounded, or missing. Many brave soldiers of both armies had to be buried near the battlefield. That's why there's a cemetery at Gettysburg.

# The Gettysburg Address

Four score and seven years ago, our fathers brought forth upon this continent, a new nation, conceived in Liberty, and dedicated to the proposition that all men are created equal.

Now we are engaged in a great civil war, testing whether that nation, or any nation so conceived and so dedicated, can long endure. We are met on a great battlefield of that war. We have come to dedicate a portion of that field, as a final resting place for those who here gave their lives that that nation might live. It is altogether fitting and proper that we should do this.

But, in a larger sense, we cannot dedicate— we cannot consecrate—we cannot hallow—this ground. The brave men, living and dead, who struggled here, have consecrated it, far above our poor power to add or detract. The world will little note, nor long remember what we say here, but it can never forget what they did here. It is for us the living, rather, to be dedicated here to the unfinished work which they who fought here have thus far so nobly advanced. It is rather for us to be here dedicated to the great task remaining before us—that from these honored dead we take increased devotion to that cause for which they gave the last full measure of devotion—that we here highly resolve that these dead shall not have died in vain—that this nation under God, shall have a new birth of freedom—and that government of the people, by the people, for the people, shall not perish from the earth.

**Abraham Lincoln,** November 19, 1863
Spoken version

Written versions

# Stop and Respond

## Speed Zones

Which parts of the story were difficult for you to understand? Did you read these difficult parts more slowly? Use self-stick notes to mark story passages that you read slowly, quickly, or at medium speed. Explain what helped you to read more quickly or what caused you to slow down. List other fix-up strategies that you used to understand difficult parts.

## You Were There

Suppose that you were asked to introduce either Edward Everett or President Lincoln at the dedication of the National Soldiers' Cemetery on November 19, 1863. What would you say? Would your introduction be long or short? Write your introduction for one of these speakers. You may want to present it to your class.

## Design a Memorial

Draw a sketch for a memorial to the soldiers who died in the Civil War. Write notes on your sketch that describe its size, the materials from which it should be constructed, and any other details about the memorial that you would like people to know.

# Helping Hands

## by Brad Herzog

Maybe it had something to do with what I dreamed the night before, although I can't quite remember what my sleeping mind imagined. Maybe it was just because I woke up in a good mood. Or maybe it was something else entirely—something I may never wholly understand—that inspired me to put my thoughts into action. Whatever the reason, I woke up that Saturday with a smile on my face and a mission on my hands.

That's my name, by the way—Sammy Hands. You can just imagine all the nicknames that go with a name like that. I've been called "Sure" Hands (when I catch the football) and "Sweaty" Hands (when I drop it). I've been known as "Clean" Hands, "No" Hands, even Sammy "Clammy" Hands.

I don't mind the nicknames at all. In fact, I think they're kind of fun. But on this particular Saturday, I wanted to be "Helping" Hands. I decided I was going to find ten people who could use a little help. And I was going to assist them. I was going to take a journey through my tiny hometown of Forest Grove, and it was

going to be a pilgrimage of peace, a voyage of value, a day of doing good.

It was easy to decide whom to help first—my mom, of course. After breakfast, I noticed a pile of dishes in the kitchen sink. Without even being asked, I began to scrub and wash and dry them. The scrubbing went great. The washing went fine. The drying? Well, that went OK until I lost my grip on a wet plate. It crashed to the floor and shattered into several pieces. Still, all in all, I think Mom was happy I helped. One down, nine to go.

I broke out my trusty scooter and wheeled my way down the sidewalk along Chestnut Street. As usual, our neighbor, Mr. Wrenn, was working on his car. Sometimes I think Mr. Wrenn fixes things that don't need fixing. But everyone needs a hobby. I decided to help him with his.

For a half hour, I stood next to Mr. Wrenn, handing him tools while he bent over the car's engine. Sure, I handed him the wrong tool once or twice. I gave him some pliers when he asked for a wrench, and I gave him a wrench when he asked for a screwdriver. But Mr. Wrenn seemed happy

What did you do when you came to *pilgrimage of peace?* How did you know what it means?

for the help. At least, he was smiling when I left.

Five houses later, I came upon Janet Steinbeck's house. Janet is in my class at school, but she wasn't home. Neither were her parents. But the Steinbeck's pet poodle, Charley, was. He was scratching at the front door and hoping to get inside.

I knew the Steinbecks always kept their door unlocked, and I sure wanted to help old Charley. So I opened the door for him. I figured the Steinbecks wouldn't mind Charley running around their house, although I did notice his paws were a little muddy. That made three good deeds already, and I hadn't even left my block yet!

I turned the corner onto Pine Avenue and made my way into the heart of Forest Grove. Pine Avenue can be a pretty busy street because it leads right to the factory at the edge of town. That makes for a lot of traffic for a little town. When I saw Mrs. Martin preparing to cross the street, I knew I had to react quickly.

Mrs. Martin is older than my mother—older than my grandmother, even. I'm not sure of her exact age, but she often talked of the days when her family would sit around the living room and listen to the radio. That seems like a long time ago. I figured Mrs. Martin shouldn't be crossing the street alone, so I ran to help her.

I made sure no cars were coming, gently took hold of her wrist, and pulled her across Pine Avenue. She sure protested a lot, but I kept telling her it was my pleasure to do such a good deed. Afterward, Mrs. Martin pointed out that we had left her shopping bag on the other side of the street. But I was happy to help again.

A little while later, I stopped in at Donna's Diner, where Donna is the only waitress. It was lunchtime, and the diner was very crowded. Boy was Donna busy! She had to hand out menus, pour drinks, take

Did you have to slow down or reread any part of this page? Why or why not?

orders, serve food, clear plates, and clean tables. If anyone could use a hand—make that Sammy Hands—it was Donna.

When I overheard a customer complain that he hadn't even had his water glass refilled, I sprang into action. I grabbed the water pitcher and hurried from table to table, filling each glass to the very top. Of course, I was a bit excited, so sometimes I filled them over the top. But at least I made Donna look good. That was my fifth helping hand of the day. I was halfway there!

As I rode my scooter along Pine Avenue, I came upon a good friend of mine, Stuart Simmons. Stuart had a scooter, too, but he was walking it. One of his wheels had broken off. Well, it just so happened that I always kept an extra wheel in my bag—just for that kind of emergency.

I helped repair Stuart's scooter, and he waved a big thank-you as he zoomed out of sight. (Later that week, I found out that Stuart would have been better off walking. He fell off his scooter and skinned his knee. But I figured that was just bad luck following a good deed.)

After turning onto Cedar Street, I nearly rolled right into a wall of fruit. There were

red apples, yellow bananas, green limes, and, well, orange oranges. This was Mr. Haywood's produce market. But the apples, oranges, bananas, and limes weren't the only fresh things at the market. Mr. Haywood was struggling to hang a freshly painted sign that said "Forest Grove Fruits."

Naturally, I had to help. I held one side of the sign and even nailed it to the wall, just as Mr. Haywood was saying, "Make sure it's straight. . . . " OK, so it wasn't all that straight. But hey, you could still read

the sign. As I scooted away, I looked over my shoulder and saw Mr. Haywood shaking his head and smiling. I'm sure he appreciated Good Deed Number Seven.

Is this what you thought the author would tell you about Mr. Haywood's actions? Why or why not?

Good Deed Number Eight came as the sun was beginning to set. As I wheeled past Mr. and Mrs. Baker's house, I saw them getting out of their car in the driveway. Mr. and Mrs. Baker had been married 50 years. That's a long marriage! In fact, they had just returned from their 50th anniversary party.

Mr. Baker was carrying a rather heavy centerpiece from the party. Mrs. Baker was carrying what was left of their anniversary

cake. Well, I figured they shouldn't have to carry anything at all. So I carried it all into the house for them. The cake got a bit squished when I put the centerpiece on top of it, but I felt I had given them the gift of a good deed.

I got home that evening and found my dad trying to fix the kitchen sink. Half of the sink was already disconnected. It was in pieces on a towel on the kitchen floor. When Dad went off to answer the phone, I felt it was my duty to help him finish taking the sink apart. So I did.

You should have seen the look on his face when he returned! I wondered if maybe he hadn't been taking apart the sink at all. Maybe he had been putting it together. But then he gave me a playful hug and said, "Sammy, I know you mean well." And I really do.

I was in bed later that night, when I realized I hadn't met my goal. I had helped nine people that day, not ten. Naturally, I was disappointed, but at the same time I felt great. In fact, my day of doing good had given me a nice, warm feeling. That's when I discovered something terrific. I was person number ten! By helping others, I had helped myself. ●

Does *By helping others, I had helped myself* make sense to you? Why or why not?

# It's All in How You Look at It

Imagine that you are one of the people in the story who was on the receiving end of Sammy Hands's good deeds. What did you think of Sammy's efforts to help you? Describe what he did for you from your point of view and how you felt about it.

# Acts of Kindness

Make a list of the ten things that Sammy did to help others. Then rank them in order from the most effective to the least effective. Pick one of Sammy's acts of kindness and tell why you think the person being helped would or would not be pleased with Sammy's efforts.

# Helping Others and Yourself

Sammy believes that by helping other people, he had helped himself. Do you agree? Discuss with a small group of classmates the ways in which helping others benefits the person who is helping as well as the people being helped. As a group, make a poster to encourage people to be kind and to help others.

## Let's Write

### Bio Poem

You are the main character. Synthesize interesting information about yourself in a Bio Poem. Use this pattern and fill in the blanks with fascinating facts about YOU!

Line 1: First and Last Name
Line 2: (Four traits that describe you) _____, _____, _____, _____
Line 3: Relative (Daughter, Son, Sister, Brother, etc.) of . . .
Line 4: Who likes _____, _____, _____ (three things or people)
Line 5: Who feels _____, _____, _____ (three items)
Line 6: Who needs _____, _____, _____ (three items)
Line 7: Who fears _____, _____, _____ (three items)
Line 8: Who gives _____, _____, _____ (three items)
Line 9: Who would like to see _____, _____, _____ (three items)
Line 10: Resident of _____
Line 11: First and Last Name

### What's in a Name?

How did you get your name? Do you know if your name has a special meaning? Ask family members if there is a "story" about why you got the name you did. Research the meaning behind your name. Share your information with the class.

### Character Sketch

Invent a character. Make a list or chart describing what the character looks like, how he or she walks and speaks, what clothes the character wears, and what the character's personality is like. Give your character a name. You may want to refer to page D17 for some ideas. Then draw a picture of your character and share it with your classmates.

## More Books

Gantos, Jack. *Joey Pigza Loses Control.* Farrar, 2000.

Kessler, Paula. *Amazing Kids.* Random House, 1995.

Krull, Kathleen. *Lives of Extraordinary Women.* Harcourt, 2000.

Levy, Elizabeth. *My Life as a Fifth-Grade Nothing.* HarperCollins, 1997.

McNulty, Faith. *With Love from Koko.* Scholastic, 1990.

Prelutsky, Jack. *It's Raining Pigs and Noodles.* Greenwillow, 2000.

## On the Web

**Gorillas/Chimps**

http://www.everwonder.com/david/gorillas

http://www.koko.org/kidsclub

http://kokomojr-tvchimp.com/todayshow.htm

**Organ Donors**

http://www.organdonor.gov

**Acts of Kindness**

http://www.actsofkindness.org

**Gettysburg Address**

http://lcweb.loc.gov/exhibits/gadd

## Across the Curriculum

### Music

Television shows—whether they're situation comedies, drama series, made-for-TV movies, or game shows—all have theme music played at their beginning and ending. Suppose you are a TV producer and have just scheduled new shows based on the four main stories you have read. Decide on appropriate theme music for each of these new shows. If possible, bring a recording of the music to class. Explain your choices to your classmates.

### Social Studies

On a map of the United States, locate the settings for the first three stories. Then decide where in the world Sammy Hands might live. Explain the reasoning for your choice and tell why you think he would be needed in this place.

# A Cast of Characters

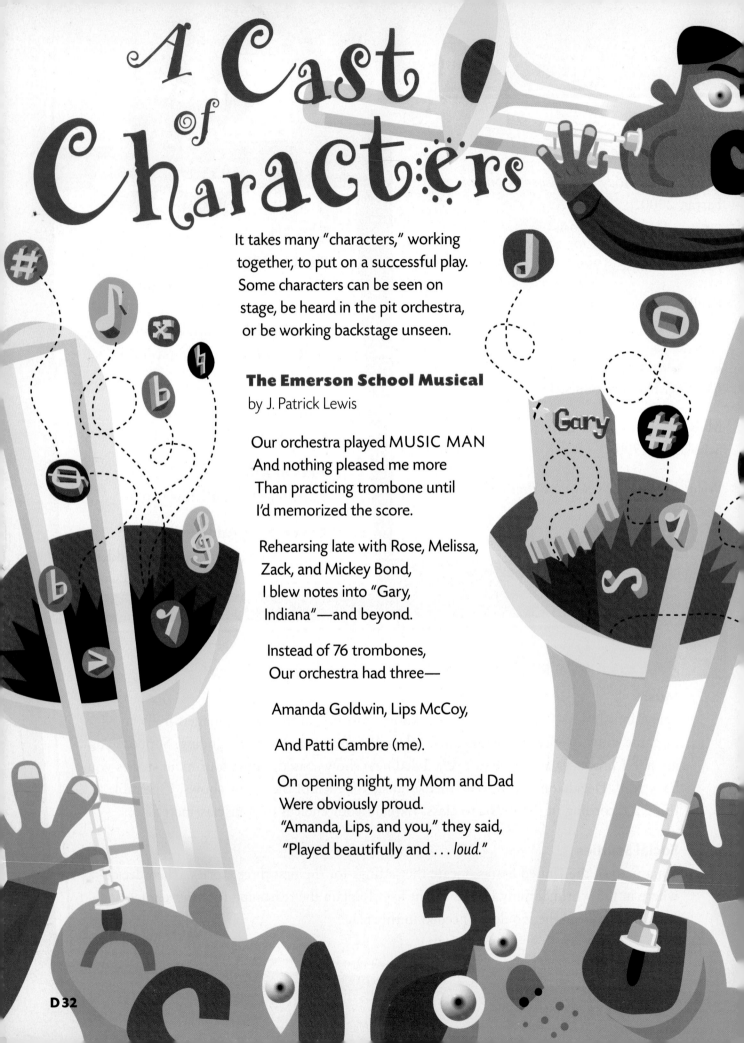

It takes many "characters," working together, to put on a successful play. Some characters can be seen on stage, be heard in the pit orchestra, or be working backstage unseen.

## The Emerson School Musical
by J. Patrick Lewis

Our orchestra played MUSIC MAN
And nothing pleased me more
Than practicing trombone until
I'd memorized the score.

Rehearsing late with Rose, Melissa,
Zack, and Mickey Bond,
I blew notes into "Gary,
Indiana"—and beyond.

Instead of 76 trombones,
Our orchestra had three—

Amanda Goldwin, Lips McCoy,

And Patti Cambre (me).

On opening night, my Mom and Dad
Were obviously proud.
"Amanda, Lips, and you," they said,
"Played beautifully and . . . *loud.*"